The Boston Celtics 1990-91 Greenbook

by Roland Lazenby

photographs by Steve Lipofsky

Celtics Profiles and Records by David Zuccaro

TAYLOR PUBLISHING COMPANY
Dallas, Texas

Design by Karen Snidow Lazenby

©1990, Roland Lazenby
Taylor Publishing Company
1550 West Mockingbird Lane, Dallas, Texas 75235

ISBN 0-87833-754-7

Printed in the United States of America

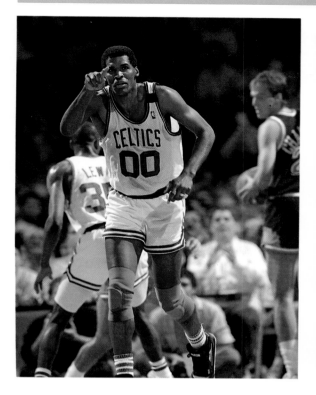

Contents

Preface

Welcome to the third editon of the *Boston Celtics Greenbook*. The upcoming season seems more promising with every passing day. Boston's hopes for 1990-91 surged in September when guard Brian Shaw decided to return to the team after a year playing in Italy.

Shaw and first-round draft pick Dee Brown should give the Celtics a depth at guard that they haven't had in a while. And new head coach Chris Ford says he is confident that they'll be very good.

Once again, many thanks are in order for this edition of the *Greenbook*. First to Tod Rosensweig, the Celtics' vice president for communications, who edited and supervised the project. And to Steve Lipofsky for his stunning photography. To David Zuccaro, the Celtics' director of publicatons and information, who authored the player bios and compiled the statistics in the back matter. Plus Jeff Twiss, the Celtics' public relations director, and Wayne Levy, the administrative assistant in public relations, were more than gracious in making sure materials and information were available.

The staff at Taylor Publishing Company did much of the yeoman's work in pushing the Greenbook along. Publisher Arnie Hanson has continued to believe in the project. Editor Jim Donovan provided the on-line editing and editorial direction. Also vital was my editorial assistant, Bob Hartman.

Beyond that, the New England newspapers again supplied their excellent coverage of the team. The list of the best should include Peter May, Jackie MacMullan and Bob Ryan at the Globe. They were excellent, as were Steve Bulpett and Mark Murphy at the Herald, and Jim Fenton at the Brockton Enterprise and Mike Fine of the Patriot Ledger. They are part of what makes Boston a great town for basketball.

The list of those granting interviews begins with Celtics President Red Auerbach, who took the time to discuss his coaching career. Others who graciously agreed to be interviewed were Chris Ford, Paul Seymour, Billy Packer, Al McGuire, Dave Gavitt, Joe Mullaney, Jan Volk, Bob Cousy, Jerry West, Elgin Baylor, Fred Schaus, Pat Riley, Gerald Henderson, and Charlie Eckman.

Extensive use was made of a variety of publications, including the *Los Angeles Times, L.A. Herald Examiner, The National, New York Daily News, The New York Times, Sports Illustrated, The Sporting News, Street & Smith's Pro Basketball Yearbook,* and *The Washington Post.*

The reporting work of a variety of writers helped tremendously: Dave Anderson, Phil Berger, Frank DeFord, Scott Ostler, Ira Berkow, Cliff Brown, Jack Madden, Tony Kornheiser, Ted Green, Mitch Chortkoff, Pat Putnam, Sandy Padwe, Jack McCallum, Sam McManis, Doug Cress, Mike Littwin, John Papanek, Leonard Lewin, Leonard Koppett, Sam Goldaper, George Vecsey, Alex Wolff, Bruce Newman.

Also, several books were keys in my research, including: *Basketball for the Player, the Fan and the Coach* by Red Auerbach; *Championship NBA* by Leonard Koppett; *College Basketball's 25 Greatest Teams* by Billy Packer and Roland Lazenby; *Cousy on the Celtic Mystique* by Bob Cousy and Bob Ryan; *Second Wind* by Bill Russell and Taylor Branch; *The Boston Celtics* by Bob Ryan; *The Modern Basketball Encyclopedia* by Zander Hollander; *The Official NBA Basketball Encyclopedia*, edited by Zander Hollander and Alex Sachare; *Winnin' Time* by Scott Ostler and Steve Springer.

The last thanks should go to the players, Robert Parish, Kevin McHale, Reggie Lewis, Michael Smith, Joe Kleine, Dave Popson, Larry Bird and Dee Brown, who took the time for interviews.

Roland Lazenby

Larry answers the questions after the '90 playoff loss.

Chris Ford takes the helm.

Going For The Glue

As youth movements go, this may not have been exactly what the fans had in mind. But youth is exactly what the Los Angeles Lakers and Boston Celtics accomplished last June when they hired rookie head coaches.

The teams' new bosses—Mike Dunleavy in Los Angeles and Chris Ford in Boston—have little or no bench experience whatsoever. Both have spent considerable time as assistant coaches, but, as Ford points out, "things change when you move over that 12 inches on the bench to the head spot."

At face value, it seems somewhat questionable. How could the National Basketball Association's most storied franchises put their fortunes in the hands of untested coaches? But face value has never mattered much with the Celtics and Lakers. Time after time, these two teams have shown a flair for taking the unorthodox and making it work. Which means there probably won't be any lines forming for people placing bets against them this time, either.

After all, it's been done before. As Lakers General Manager Jerry West points out, both Paul Westhead and Pat Riley won championships in Los Angeles as rookie head coaches.

The cynics claim that it's a players' game, so coaches aren't all that important anyway.

The reality, though, is a bit more complicated than that. Coaching does matter in the NBA, it just doesn't matter as much as it does in college. And it matters more than it ever has, because defense is more of a factor in the league today.

Coaching in the NBA, in fact, is a very fine art. There is no better example than that of the two previous coaches of the Lakers and Celtics.

"We're not interested in being competitive," Auerbach says of Ford's first Celtic team. "We're interested in winning it."

Essentially, Pat Riley is no longer in Los Angeles because he became a bit too heavy-handed in dealing with his players. They complained that he simply didn't allow them the freedom to play the game. Although they won 63 games last year, the Lakers' enthusiasm waned as the season dragged on.

"You could just see our team deteriorating," West said. "They were unhappy for a reason. I'm surprised we got past the first round."

The unhappiness among the players had been a factor for the Lakers over the past few springs, but it finally came to a head in 1990, which resulted in Riley moving on to NBC as a broadcaster.

In Boston, just the opposite scenario hurt Jimmy Rodgers. When

team dissension over Bird's shooting became a media issue last December, Celtics President Red Auerbach figured Rodgers hadn't been strong enough in dealing with the situation. When the Celtics lost to the New York Knicks in the first round of the playoffs, Auerbach and Celtics management decided to replace Rodgers after his second season on the job.

Now, in starting over with young coaches, each team is looking for something different. But they both want the same results—just the right coaching touch to coax another championship out of their rosters.

"We're not interested in being competitive," Auerbach says of Ford's first Celtic team. "We're interested in winning it."

The Lakers, of course, are taking the same approach. "Results are what we're interested in," West declared in a recent interview.

Actually, it should come as no shock that these two teams have begun their 1990s rebuilding process with a similar approach. For three decades now, the Lakers and Celtics have moved through the NBA in a lockstep, their dynasties rising and falling with an almost eerie cadence. Their first clashes came during the 1960s when the young Lakers, featuring West and Elgin Baylor, battled the Bill Russell-led Celtics. Then, in 1979, Magic Johnson and Larry Bird began moving their teams to a furious beat. Boston won three world championships in the 1980s, and Los Angeles won five.

But, as cozy as their twosome was, the Celtics and Lakers have been interrupted over the last few seasons. Neither team has won a championship in two years while the Detroit Pistons have ruled the league.

> **"In Boston, we have sophisticated fans. Their only concern is if you hang a banner up at the end of the year."**
>
> **—Chris Ford**

It's been a long time since either team has had a losing record, but merely winning isn't enough in Boston or Los Angeles.

"In Boston, we have sophisticated fans," Ford said. "Their only concern is if you hang a banner up at the end of the year."

Although he's eager to take the job, he's also very much aware that there is only so much an NBA coach can do. "There were a lot of things that arose that Jimmy had no control over," he said in Rodgers' defense.

Dealing with players in today's big-money environment will be his major challenge, Ford said. "A big key will be to get them to see what the team good is, particularly now with the lucrative contracts making it even tougher to get them to focus."

That would seem to be a pungent issue in Los Angeles because the Lakers lured unrestricted free agent forward Sam Perkins away from Dallas in August. Perkins' new six-year contract is said to run in excess of $18 million, but West hasn't even blinked at those numbers.

"They simply have to go that way when the league guarantees its players 53 percent of its revenue," he said.

Any inequities in the league's pay scale will work themselves out, West said. "We have an owner here [Dr. Jerry Buss in Los Angeles] who obviously takes care of his players."

West understandably bristles at questions about his selection of a coach. Why recycle another older coach? he asked. "We'd rather take our chances on somebody young and bright and enthusiastic and

Ford makes a point in rookie camp.

innovative, somebody you can work with."

From all accounts, the 36-year-old Dunleavy is certainly that. He has played for and served under Milwaukee coach Del Harris and Golden State's Don Nelson. That experience and his low-key but effective personal style have made him a hot property around the league. He had turned down at least two other head coaching jobs and numerous assistant offers before agreeing to join the Lakers in June.

Still, his selection was something of a surprise in Los Angeles, so Dunleavy doesn't take the questions about his lack of experience as an affront. "I take it as a compliment," he said. "They could have chosen probably anybody in the league. Anybody would have loved to have

this job. So would a lot of top college coaches. Any time there's a team with a lot of success and tradition, people want to be associated with it."

Actually both Ford and Dunleavy fit a long-established mold for coaching success. They were both "glue men" as players, valuable to their teams not as superstars but as solid, consistent performers, able to play defense and contribute just enough on offense. Glue men typically average five to 10 years in the league and score an average of seven to 12 points per game over their careers. Ford, who has the distinction of making the first three-pointer in NBA history, averaged 9.2 points a game over 10 years. For Dunleavy, who became something of a three-point specialist while playing for Philadelphia, Houston and

As a player, Ford was a glue man.

Dunleavy of the Lakers.

Milwaukee, the numbers were 8.0 points over 10 years.

A look at the honor roll of coaches who have taken teams to the Finals shows that the majority of them have a similar profile. Al Attles (8.9 points over 11 seasons), K.C. Jones (7.4 over nine seasons), Alex Hannum (6.0 over nine), Larry Costello (12.2 over 12), Pat Riley (7.4 over nine), Red Holzman (9.4 over nine), George Senesky (7.2 over eight), Paul Seymour (9.4 over 15), Fred Schaus (12.2 over five), Gene Shue (14.4 over 10), Rick Adelman (7.7 over seven) and Al Cervi (9.4 over 9) were all relatively average players who went on to accomplish great things as coaches. Between them, the teams they coached have made 31 trips to the Finals and come away with 14 championships.

The reasons that glue men make good coaches are fairly obvious, Dunleavy said. "More than likely, they've had to survive and succeed on more than athletic ability."

"We were probably sound fundamentally although we weren't superstars," Ford agreed.

They were the kinds of players who had to know their team's system inside and out, Dunleavy said, and they had to play defense. Because they weren't always as quick, they had to know the opponent's systems and tendencies. "I had to know where my guy was going before he made his move," Dunleavy said.

As a result of the extra work they put in, the glue men got a complete look at the game, which meant they had the basic knowledge to become coaches. They had learned to

formulate their ideas and copy from others.

Also, average players tend to move around in their careers, which means they see a variety of coaching styles. "I played for eight different coaches in 10 years," Ford said. The list runs from K.C. Jones to Dick Vitale, and Ford said he has learned from all of them.

The main lesson?

"You need a great working relationship with the players," he said.

Ford's confidence seems high heading into the season despite the difficult circumstances of his hiring. He had to wait while Auerbach and Dave Gavitt, Boston's new man in charge of basketball operations, considered a list of candidates, including Duke coach Mike Krzyzewski, to run the Celtics. The Celtic players and the Boston media all lobbied for Ford, and eventually he got the job.

Despite those circumstances, the 41-year-old Ford hardly sees himself as either a second choice or a rookie. "I've been in this game 18 years now," he said. "I've been on the down side and the up side and whatever. This is my 13th year with the Celtics. I think I'm ready."

The Celtics do, too. Gavitt figures the team has played without fire and intensity the past few seasons. "I think we've lost a little feistiness in recent years," he said. "We've lost a little competitiveness."

Ford played with them way back when they did have those qualities, namely in 1981 when they won a world championship on their

The Celtics have gotten Shaw off the sideline.

chutzpah. He was also an assistant coach to K.C. Jones on the 1984 and '86 championship teams. His main challenge will be to rekindle that old fire.

"We used to have a cockiness to us," Ford said, "a belief that we were invincible. You could sense it."

He recalled that former Celtic Cedric Maxwell used to sit in the locker room before away games and ask how many seats had been sold. "Somebody would tell him 17,000 or whatever the number was," Ford said, "and Max would say, 'Well, we're gonna send 17,000 people home unhappy tonight.' That was the feeling we had, the cockiness. The Pistons have had that for the past few seasons. They'll do whatever it takes to win."

"Cedric was funny," agreed former Celtic Gerald Henderson. "He was cocky. Our whole team was cocky."

Boston's choice of coaches was right on the mark, said Henderson,

Ford's former teammate. "I think the guys respect Chris a lot. He's got a good temperament for that position. Of course, you don't know how his X's and O's are gonna be. He's never been in that position before. But I think he'll be good for the team."

In addition to firing up the veterans, Ford is faced with encouraging his younger players to improve, which isn't always easy in the NBA fast lane. "There are some guys here who don't attack their games and try to improve them," he said. "That's the hazard of long-term contracts."

West, though, says a coach can't bear too much of the responsibility. It's a players' game, and ultimately the players will determine the team's success, he said. "A coach is an important factor in a championship team, but not the most important factor. You have to have the players."

In that sense, the pressure is on the Lakers' front office, not Dunleavy,

to get the players, West said. "If we can bring him the right people, then he should have a good chance for success."

To that end, West made a series of dazzling roster moves during the offseason. Unsure that he would make the team, veteran guard Michael Cooper moved on to play in Italy, and West dealt backup forward Orlando Woolridge to Denver.

Those moves created room enough in the salary cap to allow him to sign Perkins and maybe do even more. In fact, the Lakers still have a bit of room under their cap and at press time were shopping for another guard or any deal that would make them better.

The circumstances mean that Dunleavy's challenge will be quick assembly. He'll have to get them all playing together quickly. Going into the season, he plans to start second-year Yugoslavian center Vlade Divac with A.C. Green and James Worthy in

In addition to Shaw, first-round draft pick Dee Brown of Jacksonville could bring the team some quickness and depth at guard.

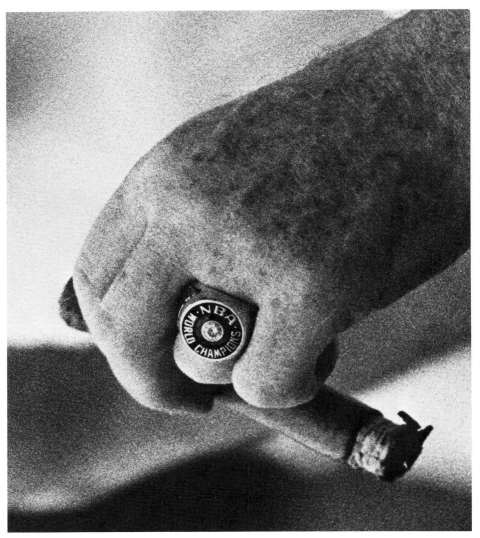

Red wants another ring.

the frontcourt, while bringing the $18-million Perkins off the bench.

"It's a matter of how quickly we can bring it all together," Dunleavy said.

Two weaknesses emerged last season with the Lakers. They struggled to score with their half-court offense, and on defense they were vulnerable to smaller, quicker guards. People in Los Angeles have been reluctant to say it, but Dunleavy isn't. The Lakers missed Kareem Abdul-Jabbar, who retired after the 1989 season, he said. "I think there was a void there. Basically with Kareem in your lineup, you could always get a shot."

The 6'9" Perkins won't solve that problem by himself, but the Lakers see him as a marvelously versatile player, capable of playing power forward, center or small forward.

The Celtics, meanwhile, have been faced with one of the tightest salary caps in the league. They moved cautiously in the offseason, spending their time trying to lure holdout point guard Brian Shaw back into the Boston fold. They were rewarded in mid-September when Shaw announced that he was not only ready but eager to return.

Like that, the Celtics got back the point guard they missed so badly in 1989-90, a factor that will greatly improve Ford's chances for success. Shaw, who averaged 8.6 points per game as a starter his rookie season with the Celtics, played for Il Messagaro in Italy last season, leading the team in both scoring and rebounding.

In addition to Shaw, first-round draft pick Dee Brown of Jacksonville

could bring the team some quickness and depth at guard.

"I think things will be really positive with Dee Brown and Brian Shaw bringing speed and defense to the lineup," Ford said. "Plus the veterans have something to prove after getting knocked out of the playoffs. Larry is fully recovered [from heel surgery that forced him to sit out most of the '89 season] and his legs are in good shape."

Kevin McHale agreed. "There's a big challenge ahead of us," the Boston forward said, "and I think part of that challenge has been met by the organization, by hiring Chris and Gavitt, the change in the front office. So now we have to meet the challenge as players and prove our game."

Even as Ford speaks positively, he

knows that he and Dunleavy, two former long-range gunners, are now faced with a short-range hustle. That doesn't seem to bother either one of them.

Ford recalled that as a starter for Boston he faced Dunleavy, then playing for Houston, in the 1981 Finals. "We both had nice careers, and we played against each other in the Finals," Ford said. "Fortunately my team won. Hopefully we'll get to meet there again."

"I'd go for that," Dunleavy said in a blink.

Spoken, perhaps, with the youthful enthusiasm of rookies, but heading into the '90s that may be just what these two teams need.

Ford wants to see the Celtics play with their old fire.

Magic and Bird were glad to be back at it after Larry's year off.

Shoot, Larry

While his career has been nothing short of remarkable, Larry Bird was faced with a difficult set of circumstances for the 1989-90 season. He returned to pro basketball after a year's layoff while recovering from career-threatening surgery to remove bone spurs from both of his heels.

To say the least, expectations were tremendous.

His comeback trail had its share of strange twists and uneven turns. First, there were the numerous delays to his planned return, originally set for the spring of 1989. When he finally made it back to active duty in the Boston Celtics rookie camp over the summer, he played only a matter of minutes before fracturing a small bone in his back in a collision with another player.

He shook off that scare only to encounter a new round of troubles once the season began. The year off had left him rusty, as evidenced by his inconsistent shooting over the first third of the schedule, and that led to a thorough media investigation of his abilities.

"What's Wrong With Larry?" *Sports Illustrated* asked in

Deadeye.

The early, high-flying Bird.

an early-season cover story.

One writer wondered if Bird was worried about the situation. "I don't have to do that 'cause you do it for me," he replied. "Everybody worries about my shooting but me."

Looking at the statistics, you might wonder what all the fuss was about. A 50-percent shooter over his career, Bird hit 47 percent of his shots for the season, about the same as his old foe, Magic Johnson.

"I'm not gonna worry about it at all," Robert Parish said of Bird's shooting. "When his shot isn't going, he always does the other things, rebounding, passing. That's why he's such a great ballplayer."

Over the season, Bird averaged 24.3 points, 9.5 rebounds and 7.5 assists. His performance included 10 triple doubles. At one point, he made 71 consecutive free throws, the second-longest streak in NBA history, and he finished with the league's best free-throw percentage (.930).

Larry went on a particularly torrid run after the All-Star break. Over the 15 games from February 21 to March 23, he hit 172 of 313 shots from the field (55 percent) and averaged 28.5 points, 11 rebounds and seven assists per game.

Asked by a reporter about the criticism he had received, Bird replied, "One thing about the NBA, when you read the papers, everybody wants you to score 30 and 35 points like you used to. If you don't hit the shots, you're not gonna do that. But this is a scoring league. If I didn't get but three rebounds and three assists and averaged 35 points, everybody would be thinking I had a great year."

Asked if the situation was the most frustrating he'd faced since coming into the league in 1979, Bird said that things had been pretty rosy for him over the years. "I'm just glad to be back playing," he said. "I'd play in Puerto Rico if they'd let me."

There's no need to play in Puerto Rico, Larry. Your style works just fine in Boston. As the accompanying photographs show, you're the ultimate competitor.

So shoot. And play your game. The rest will take care of itself.

The Bird fire.

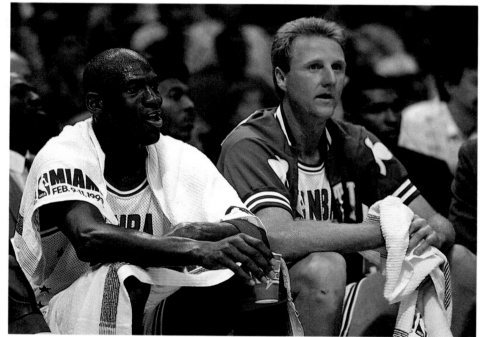

Larry and Mike take an All-Star break.

Bird through the years.

Larry loosens up.

Looking for a board.

The competitor.

Directing traffic.

Gavitt with Rudy LaRusso at Dartmouth.

Dave Gavitt's New Game

I t was the kind of career move that left old friends puzzled and surprised.

When Joe Mullaney heard last spring that Dave Gavitt was resigning as commissioner of the Big East Conference to head up basketball operations for the Boston Celtics, he had just one question.

Why?

Why would Gavitt, one of the most powerful, successful men in college basketball, give all that up for the difficult challenges of the NBA?

Al McGuire, the NBC broadcaster who was Gavitt's freshman coach at Dartmouth in 1955, wondered too. "I think he's probably taken on his greatest challenge with the Celtics," McGuire said.

When Mullaney, an old friend and former boss of Gavitt's, spoke with him after the announcement, Gavitt seemed almost sheepish, Mullaney said. "He really didn't say why. His opening line to me was, 'I guess you were surprised.' I said I certainly was."

During their conversation, which occurred at Big East offices, Gavitt "never did define exactly why he made the move," Mullaney said.

Mullaney, by the way, knows all the parties well.

He certainly knows college basketball, having coached many years at Providence College.

And he has more than a little experience with the pro game, too. He coached the Los Angeles Lakers to the NBA Finals in 1970, where they lost in seven games to Willis Reed and the New York Knicks. And he

Dave Gavitt is a yankee's yankee. He worked his way to the top of the basketball world over the past three decades without ever leaving his native New England.

directed the Kentucky Colonels to a 68-win season in the old American Basketball Association. Mullaney, who played his college ball with Bob Cousy at Holy Cross, even played a season (1949-50) for the Celtics.

So Joe knows pro ball.

He knows all about the frustrations of the game, about trying to deal with big egos and agents and playing-time hassles.

"Dave, it's a different world," Mullaney recalled telling Gavitt. "You just don't have the control you'd like to have. You're dealing with professional players. You just don't have the leverage. In high school and college coaching, you run the show. But not in the pros."

Mullaney knows Dave Gavitt, too. He gave him his first college coaching job as an assistant at Providence. He watched Gavitt grow from coach to creator of a super conference to the man who directed college basketball toward its golden television bonanza.

Most important, Mullaney over the years has come to know this about Dave Gavitt:

"He isn't gonna make any stupid moves, that's for sure."

THE RISING STAR

Dave Gavitt is a yankee's yankee. He worked his way to the top of the basketball world over the past three decades without ever leaving his native New England.

He spent much of his childhood—during and immediately after World War II—in Westerly, Rhode Island, where the local high school team sparked his fascination with the game. At the same time, the University of Rhode Island's high-scoring team with Ernie Calverley was attracting national attention. To a grade-schooler like Gavitt, it seemed that the basketball world revolved around Rhode Island.

"I really got hooked on the game," he said.

But when Gavitt was in the sixth grade, his family moved to Peterborough, New Hampshire. His heart, though, remained with Westerly and Rhode Island basketball.

"I went to this small town in New Hampshire, and they had a hockey team," he recalled. "But I never thought about playing hockey." He stayed with basketball and baseball and matured into a star at Peterborough High. As a teen-ager, he also took an interest in the Celtics, where Auerbach was trying to build a winner.

"Red was just getting started with Cousy and Ed Macauley," Gavitt said.

Gavitt thinks the Celtics' veterans are part of the solution.

He graduated from high school in 1955 and went to Dartmouth to play for former Celtic coach Doggie Julian. Before he got to Julian, though, Gavitt played a year on the freshman team for a rooster of a coach, Al McGuire.

"Dave was a heady player. Chunky. Round," McGuire recalled with a laugh. "Could hit the outside shot. Team-oriented. He had a leadership quality about him. He wasn't a holler-type guy. Not a lot of rah-rah. Just quiet leadership."

A ballhandling guard, Gavitt combined with 6'8" Rudy LaRusso to give Dartmouth three excellent varsity teams from 1957-59. Over Gavitt's three varsity seasons, the Big Green racked up a 62-18 record and battled their way as far as the East Regional Final in 1958.

"I was fortunate to play at Dartmouth when we had Rudy LaRusso, who was a terrific player," Gavitt said. "We won three out of four Ivy League championships."

LaRusso, of course, went on to notoriety with the Lakers, and Gavitt, who had also lettered three years in baseball, took a job at Worcester (Mass.) Academy as baseball coach and assistant basketball coach.

Then in 1962, after two years at Worcester, Mullaney brought him to Providence. It was just the fast track that Gavitt needed. His official title was the freshman coach. In those days, Mullaney says, the assistants were often assigned the freshman team, which meant that they got plenty of bench coaching experience while doing the assistant's chores. Today, Mullaney says, college assistants don't get that experience and often are promoted to head coaching jobs with no time on the bench. Gavitt, however, showed pretty quickly that he knew how to work a game.

His prize as a young coach was a freshman group that included future pros Mike Riordan, Dexter Westbrook and Jimmy Walker, a team that went undefeated. "They were very, very good," Mullaney said.

"It was obvious that he was gifted from day one," Mullaney said of Gavitt. Particularly with people and

Dave and Red go way back.

ideas. He could mix the two and make something happen. And he could handle a variety of tasks at once. Even as he worked as Mullaney's assistant, he coached baseball in the Cape League and served as Providence's varsity tennis coach. During the fall, he was general manager of the Providence Steamrollers, a semi-professional football team.

After four years at Providence, he moved to Dartmouth as head coach for a season and a half. Then in 1969, when Mullaney agreed to coach the Lakers, Gavitt took over the Providence program. His first team went 14-11, then the Friars headed into a string of 20-win seasons.

Gavitt's 1973 team, featuring Ernie DiGregorio, Kevin Stacom and Marvin Barnes, went 27-4 and made it to the

Final Four in St. Louis. The Friars even led Memphis State by nine at the half. But then Barnes injured his leg, and Providence lost the opportunity to meet Bill Walton and UCLA for the national championship.

Regardless, the 37-year-old Gavitt had established his reputation as one of the best young minds in basketball. From 1969-79, he ran up a 227-117 record and was voted New England Coach of the Year five times.

When asked about Gavitt's coaching success, CBS broadcaster Billy Packer, who knows Gavitt well, said with tongue in cheek that it must be due to the year he spent with McGuire.

More seriously, Packer said Gavitt reminded him of Rollie Massimino or Dean Smith. "He was very thorough," Packer said. "A solid tactician. He could orchestrate the action."

For years, Northeastern coaches had talked about forming some type of high-profile conference, but it was Gavitt who finally got the job done in 1979 with the establishing of the Big East Conference.

Two years after taking the Providence coaching job, Gavitt was named the school's athletic director. And, as he had in the past, he quickly proved he was capable of handling the multiple duties. His team prospered and so did Providence athletics.

For years, Northeastern coaches had talked about forming some type of high-profile conference, but it was Gavitt who finally got the job done in 1979 with the establishing of the Big East Conference. It was a stroke of marketing/basketball genius. The conference was comprised mostly of small and mid-sized schools. But they were in all the major Eastern media markets. St. John's in New York. Boston College. Georgetown in Washington. Villanova in Philadelphia. Pittsburgh. To go with them were the competitive spices of Syracuse, Seton Hall, Providence and the University of Connecticut.

It translated into instant, overwhelming success. In the league's first 10 seasons, Big East teams made eight trips to the Final Four and won two NCAA championships. The conference was not only competitive, it was a natural for television, which meant fat broadcasting paychecks for the member schools.

"It was his baby from the beginning," Mullaney said. "He really orchestrated the whole thing."

Pulling the schools together and getting them to agree had been a tremendous undertaking, but Gavitt was able to do it, Mullaney said. "He's a great mediator."

For example, Mullaney recalled that Helen Bert, the former

Gavitt with John Thompson at the 1984 Final Four, with broadcasters Billy Packer and Gary Bender in the background.

administrator for women's athletics at Providence, was a fan of Gavitt's. "She used to tell me that she'd go storming into Dave's office angry over something," Mullaney said. "Dave would take time to talk over things. She'd come out and say, 'I didn't get what I wanted, but I feel a lot better.' Dave has a way of pulling people together."

Those skills were especially useful in forming the Big East, in getting big-name coaches to overcome their fears and natural competitive urges. Watching the conference grow from the beginning was special, Gavitt said. "You know it's your child, and you kind of raise it and you do take special pride in it."

But he holds no illusion that the job was something he accomplished alone. "The Big East wouldn't have worked without some key people," he said. "The coaches were critical, and the fact we were able to get schools to cooperate willingly in a very competitive atmosphere is always significant."

His abilities, however, reached far beyond a single conference. Even before his success with the Big East, Gavitt was named to the NCAA Basketball Tournament Committee in 1978. The committee is responsible for negotiating television rights fees and selecting the teams each year for the tournament. Named the committee's chairman in 1981, Gavitt was directly responsible for negotiating dramatic increases in the monies paid for broadcast rights to the NCAA tournament.

He was able to do so because he understood television almost as well as he understood basketball. "He has as much if not more overall knowledge of intercollegiate athletics and all of its applications than anyone I've ever met," said Packer of CBS. "He's a great listener and developer of ideas. And unlike a lot of people, he can get them implemented."

McGuire, NBC's college basketball analyst, says he has been amazed

The crewcut Gavitt (right) as a young Dartmouth coach.

Gavitt helped create the college hoops expansion.

Like Auerbach, Gavitt was bright and ambitious and saw tremendous promise in the game.

Best as Gavitt can figure, they probably met in 1964 when he was an assistant at Providence and Auerbach was working on drafting the Friars' young center, John Thompson.

Like Auerbach, Gavitt was bright and ambitious and saw tremendous promise in the game. Auerbach has often said that he is suspicious of people, particularly braggarts who spent their time talking about their accomplishments. Gavitt, though, was different. He talked little about himself.

"After a period of time—while I coached at Providence in the '70s—Red and I became good friends," Gavitt said. "We have always kind of had a unwritten agreement with each other: I would never call him for tickets unless they were for myself, and the same with him. So we ended up being ticket buddies. I would come out and see some Celtics games, and I would get him tickets to the Final Four. You know, over a period of time we had a lot of mutual good friends. Cousy, Heinsohn, Havlicek—people who played for him—and John Thompson."

Last December, long before anyone ever thought about Gavitt joining the Celtics, Gavitt phoned Auerbach to exercise his ticket-buddy option. He wanted to see the Celtics/Lakers game.

"One of my good friends is Vic Bubas, the former great coach at Duke," Gavitt said. "We have shared a lot of common time on the NCAA committee and done some other things together. Vic and his wife came up for a few days and we went to the Celtics/Lakers game. Vic had

watching Gavitt develop and grow over the years. "He seems to be able to move an audience, a conference, or a league without a lot of glitter," McGuire said. "He's almost mundane. Of all the people involved, you would think he has the least to say."

Perhaps that is why Packer's compliment—he says Gavitt's the "best committee member I've ever seen"—carries such ironic humor. But as bland as it sounds, Gavitt's low-key operating style has created a success that speaks for itself. Not many people aspire to be great committee members, but then again not many people have accomplished what Gavitt has.

Packer said he can't think of a major figure in college basketball today who doesn't have a genuine respect for Gavitt. His abilities have

impressed the international basketball community as well, Packer said. Gavitt was the U.S. Olympic coach for 1980, the year that President Jimmy Carter order a boycott of the games. He is currently president of USA Basketball, the organization that oversees America's Olympic efforts, and as such has many friends and acquaintances around the world.

Which only makes Mullaney all the more curious as to why he decided to take on the NBA challenge.

GHOSTS

Dave Gavitt doesn't remember exactly when he first met Red Auerbach.

"I honestly don't," he says. "It seems like I've known Red all my life."

Boston needs more Reggies, Gavitt says.

never been in the Garden."

Before the game, they stopped by the Celtics' offices. "We went in Red's office, and Red was great. And when we went into the building Vic's eyes opened and he said, 'Oh my god, there are ghosts in here.' "

Gavitt could sense the ghosts, too. The banners. The parquet. The retired numbers. He had been to the Garden many times, but each time he returned he found the atmosphere impressive.

Auerbach doesn't exactly remember when he came up with the idea of getting Dave Gavitt to run the Celtics. But the team's future had been playing on his mind for some time. And the December visit probably got him to thinking.

The thought returned after the Celtics closed their season with a disappointing loss to the Knicks in the playoffs. Auerbach said that as soon as he mentioned the idea of Gavitt to team owners Alan Cohen and Don

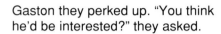

"Dave is a patient administrator. He builds for a solid foundation as opposed to a quick fix. He did that as a coach and as an administrator."

—Billy Packer

Gaston they perked up. "You think he'd be interested?" they asked.

THE SUPERIOR PATIENCE

Red Auerbach has been known for his slick personnel moves over the years. But he thinks he made his slickest in May 1990 when he brought in the 54-year-old Gavitt.

"There's no doubt about it," he said with typical Auerbachian pride. "That was my idea."

The Celtics president sees it as the first big step in retooling for the future. "You gotta do it at the top first," he explained, "then you move down."

While Gavitt is considered to be the man who revolutionized college basketball, he hasn't come to Boston with any revolutions in mind.

"Dave is a patient administrator," observed Packer. "He builds for a solid foundation as opposed to a quick fix. He did that as a coach and as an administrator. And I think he'll do it for the Celtics.

"He's not the kind of guy who will try to come in and sweep the world off its feet. That's just not the way he operates."

And that is just why Auerbach rests easier about turning over the baby he has nourished for the past 40 years.

"He's got patience and that's important," Auerbach said. "Not only that, he has knowledge, and he has it from all sides, as a player, a coach, an administrator, a businessman."

There was speculation that the Celtics made the move for Gavitt because of their loss to New York in

Gavitt, the young head coach.

Gavitt's brainchild, the Big East, has quickly become a great conference.

the playoffs, but Auerbach said that wasn't the case. "We'd been talking about it for quite awhile," he said. "We would have done it regardless of the outcome."

The 74-year-old Auerbach, who lives in Washington, said the motivation was simple. He didn't want to spend as much time in Boston. Over the past two seasons, there has been criticism that Auerbach wasn't spending enough time there. With Gavitt in charge of basketball operations, that criticism is no longer valid.

Unfortunately, Gavitt's introduction to Boston was complicated by the hiring of a coach following the release of Jimmy Rodgers. Assistant Chris Ford was the top candidate, but the Celtics lingered over their decision while taking time to discuss the job with Duke coach Mike Krzyzewski.

Krzyzewski later removed his name from consideration, a move that led to press reports that Auerbach and Gavitt were in disagreement just days after Gavitt had come to work for the Celtics.

Gavitt later denied any disagreement, but he admitted that the search for a new coach had been too painful and too public. "It was tough," he said, "because Chris had been waiting out there for four weeks already."

Ford says that Gavitt talked with him daily during the eight days Auerbach and Gavitt deliberated over the coaching choice. "I understand the process they had to go through with Dave being new on the job," Ford said. "Dave doesn't move hastily. He likes to evaluate, to get to the root of the problem. He talked to me throughout the process. I was confident in how he was going to handle the situation."

The coaching selection was followed by a series of events—the draft, the Celtics various court battles over players' rights, the preparations for rookie camp—which made Gavitt's first two months on the job a bit hectic.

But those challenges only served to whet his appetite, and he said he has complete confidence in his new situation.

"The relationship with Red has been wonderful for me," he said in July. "It has been a great learning experience. I wouldn't have taken this job unless I had a real good relationship with Red and if I hadn't gotten the proper assurances contractually from the owners that my authority and responsibility would be balanced."

The operating guidelines for the Celtics are simple, he added. "Whatever Red wants to be is how it should be. He has earned that right over 40 years. The working relationship that I have had with Red for the first seven weeks has been terrific. The media would like to make other of it. But that's simply not the fact, and the media's interpretation of it is not bothersome to Red or myself."

He was awed that Auerbach would approach him about taking the job, he said. "I felt proud that Red would approach me about it, that I was someone he would pass the baton to at the appropriate time. Red is just an unbelievable resource even though he's not—by his own admission, nor should anybody expect him to be—involved on a daily basis as much as he once was. He nonetheless is a fountain of information and just has tremendous insight into the league. Although he may not be totally current on every single player, he's a great insurance policy for me. I have sensed that already. You run things by him, and he's going to prevent you from making a serious mistake."

Gavitt making mistakes is not what concerns Joe Mullaney. "He's not gonna make mistakes, he's not gonna give away the store," the

The new Celtic braintrust—Dave, Red, and Jan.

Gavitt is impressed with McHale.

Gavitt ponders his first draft.

retired Providence coach said. "Still, there are no guarantees of championships three years down the road."

THE CHALLENGE

The appeal of the Celtics, with their New England tradition, proved strong for Gavitt.

"No disrespect intended," he said, "But we're talking geography and tradition. I don't know that I would have dropped what I was doing and gone to Sacramento or Seattle or Milwaukee. I think the Celtics being who they were and Red approaching me initially made the difference."

Plus, he had known Alan Cohen for years and felt comfortable with the team's ownership.

A big factor, McGuire suspects, was the opportunity. After years of taking care of the financial well-being of college basketball, it was finally time for Dave Gavitt to secure his personal well-being.

"If you work in the academic community and they give you $110,000 per year, they think they're giving you the campus," McGuire said. "Dave had never really rung the register, so to speak. You can't do that in college without looking like you got your hand in the cookie jar."

The money of the NBA has its appeal, but Gavitt's friends and associates figure the biggest reason he took the Celtics job was the challenge.

Mullaney speculated that maybe the Big East had become old hat to Gavitt, that maybe he thought that he had accomplished all he could in that job.

"I think Dave looks for new challenges," agreed Billy Packer. "He had accomplished everything at the Big East."

If Gavitt was looking for a challenge, he certainly found one in the Celtics, McGuire said. "Dave is a leader. I always think of a leader as someone who solves major problems. They take care of the earthquakes and the wars and the famines. If he solves the Boston Celtics, I'll kneel down and kiss his ring. He's

McGuire was Gavitt's freshman coach at Dartmouth.

Doggie Julian, the former Celtic coach, coached Dave at Dartmouth.

automatically a bishop if he does that."

Mullaney agreed: "He's got an aging team, which means he faces some tough choices."

Gavitt acknowledges that he faces a challenge, but he sees it differently: "As I said the day I was hired, my own belief is that we are not as good as we were. We're not number one or two in the league like we were for years with the Lakers, and we're not as bad as the media or conventional wisdom would have us be. We're sure not as good as we want to be. How we get there is tough, and everyone in the organization understands that, from the owners to Red and everyone else. Rules have changed with the salary cap and restricted free agency and all the other things. But it can be done, and we've got a terrific nucleus.

"I've been amused by the fact that people want to point to our veteran players, who are great players—Larry and Robert and Kevin in particular— as our problem. They are not our problem. Our problem is that we are not deep enough or solid enough around them. We need more Reggie Lewises. There are a couple of ways that can happen. You can develop the young players you have now and make them better. You can draft real well, which we hope we've done with Dee Brown, and build it block by block that way. Or you can make some roster moves that force it to happen. None of those is easy."

Many observers have pointed out over the years that the Celtics have prospered on the luck of the Irish. Auerbach himself has attributed the team's success to a strong mix of hard work and luck.

Gavitt admits that a streak of good breaks would be welcomed. "You probably have to be fortunate somewhere along the line," he says. At the same time, he doesn't plan to bank the team's future on mere chance.

"The image has been that there was always an element of luck in Red's success in Boston," Packer said. "Whether Dave has that same luck, we'll soon find out. But none of

Gavitt loves the garden atmosphere.

Gavitt as Big East commissioner.

team. And he had a message for them as well.

"I've had great conversations with most of our players, not all of them, but most of them, and long conversations with Larry and Kevin, two of the real key players," he said. "I think we've lost a little feistiness in recent years. We've lost a little competitiveness. We just have to get hungrier. I think the appetite is there. When you talk to Kevin and Larry the thing they want to do most is win. They are true professionals and great players, and so is Robert. I have not had a chance to talk to him yet, but he obviously fits in the same mold. Extremely proud and very motivated. I think that's where Chris Ford is going to make a big difference. I think Chris is going to demand that those competitive fires be lit and lit brightly."

THE FEEL

Another part of the challenge will be Gavitt's own development as a pro basketball manager. That isn't the part of the equation that concerns Joe Mullaney. "Everything he's ever taken on in life he knew he'd be successful at because he's very competent," Mullaney said. "He knew he'd do well as a head coach because he could recruit and work the bench. He didn't know he'd go to the Final Four, but he knew he'd be a winner."

The same was true with administration, Mullaney said. Gavitt knew he had the people skills to be successful.

But pro basketball is different.

"I told him he was taking a road," Mullaney said, "where all of your experience, all of your ability, all of your intelligence may not get the job done the way you'd like."

His great way with people will probably mean that Gavitt will find success in pro basketball, Mullaney said. "He hadn't been at the job but a couple of weeks when he had already talked with Dennis Johnson. Dave makes a point of touching base with people and listening to their opinions. But when you sit down with an agent and a player, it's a different ball game. You're not just bringing two

his success in the past was achieved with luck. Everything Dave has done in the past has been achieved with hard work and understanding. There is a sense now that the Celtics are on a run of bad luck. First there was the death of Len Bias, then Larry Bird's heel surgery, and later the contract dispute with Brian Shaw. If that's bad luck, I feel sure Dave will change it. Not with good luck, but with his old standbys—work and understanding."

Gavitt has wasted little time in employing those properties during his first few months on the job. "I am

happy with the start we've made," he said. "I think we got a great draft choice and I think we made a great choice in Chris Ford, who will work hard to develop and challenge younger players."

Gavitt's major strength over the years has been his ability to communicate with people one on one. He made a point of doing that not long after he arrived in Boston. His first contacts included Larry Bird and Kevin McHale. Gavitt has a reputation as a good listener. He wanted to hear their opinions on the people together. It's adversarial. It's a hardball situation."

Gavitt, of course, has played quite a bit of hardball during his career. His amiable exterior covers an underlying toughness.

"He never shows emotion outwardly," McGuire said, "but inside is a tiger that's a fierce competitor."

Perhaps his main asset will be his quick mind. He has to learn the business quickly. Although he's been a Celtics fan since high school, Gavitt said he hasn't actually paid much attention to pro basketball over the years "other than to watch Celtic successes in the playoffs."

He has developed more of an interest in the the NBA over the past decade, he said. "The league has really matured. The level of coaching is outstanding. The administration of the league overall by Commissioner Stern is unequalled in sport at any level."

His first challenge, he says, will be "acquiring a feel for the game and a feel for the process and the way the league runs. The rules within the league in terms of salary cap and other things that [Celtics General Manager] Jan Volk is very adept at.

"Roster management is a technique that I need to learn. I have a good feel for some people in the league, but I don't have a feel for all of them. It's the people that are the bottom line. And I'm looking forward to it. I know an awful lot of people in the NBA that I have dealt with over the years."

In fact, if he is to bring immediate change to Boston, it will be in the Celtics' relations around the league. "I think because of the Celtics' success over the years, it was not the most popular franchise in the league," Gavitt said frankly. "I don't think you can win a title 16 times without having some feelings hurt along the way. They may have been exasperated by the cigar smoke."

Perhaps if they had lost a little more they'd be a little more popular, Gavitt said. But he doesn't want that type of popularity. Still, he does have solid relationships with some old Celtic foes.

"I went to Chicago for the pre-draft meetings with a lot of our people," Gavitt said, "but I was introducing them to as many people as they were introducing to me, which kind of surprised me."

Better communications certainly won't hurt Boston's ability to deal. After years of being burned by Auerbach's craftiness, some NBA executives are reluctant to talk trades.

Now Gavitt will spearhead a new Celtic triumvirate. Gavitt will run the basketball operations. General Manager Jan Volk, a lawyer, is as well-versed as anyone in the myriad contractual web surrounding NBA deals. And Auerbach, of course, will continue to provide the long view.

"They are both tremendous resources in their own way," Gavitt said of Volk and Auerbach. "Jan has done a terrific job with the Celtics in his role, and I see him continuing in that role, running the club on a day-to-day basis, being my right hand with the business operations of the ball club."

As a native New Englander, Gavitt heads into his first Celtic season with a strong sense of the team's tradition. It may take time, but he wants to build a future for that tradition. He wants to make sure the Celtics aren't merely clinging to the symbols of a glorious past.

In a sense, the team's move to a new Boston Garden, projected for the 1993-94 season, will aid him in that transition. The new building will require a renewed committment to excellence.

"The best way to preserve any tradition is to win," Gavitt said. "It would be nice to project having a good team in '93-94. That's the first and foremost thing. When we move into the new building some of the old symbols of tradition will go along. The parquet will go with us, the banners will go with us, and hopefully Red will go with us and be as feisty and fearsome as ever."

If nothing else, it's a clear vision of the Celtics' future, and that should sell well in Boston.

Gavitt is already comfortable in Boston.

The young wolves at rookie camp.

Kevin Goes To Camp

There are a few good reasons for a superstar to avoid a rookie/free agent camp. After all, who wants to dine with a bunch of hungry wolves? They snap and scrap for every morsel, every loose rebound. They foul. They woof. They'll do anything to impress the coaches.

For a variety of reasons, Kevin McHale decided to show up at the Celtics' rookie camp at Babson College in Wellesley this past July. And he not only dined with the wolves. He even showed them how to cut up their steak. Not the polite way, mind you. The NBA way. A thigh here. An elbow there.

As starved as the wolves were for opportunity, they were just as hungry to peek into McHale's bag of low-post tricks. And he was just gracious enough to show them.

The camp featured about 16 free agents hoping to win an invitation to Boston's training camp in October, where they would face an even slimmer chance of earning a roster spot. To go with the free agents were about the same number of college undergraduates, eager to learn a little about the pro game and maybe impress the pro scouts for future consideration. Among the big-name college players to show up were LeRon Ellis of Syracuse and Matt Geiger of Georgia Tech.

In addition to McHale, a variety of Celtic regulars made an appearance. Reggie Lewis was the only other starter. But Charles Smith and John Bagley, who will be battling for spots on the roster, attended, as did Michael Smith, who needed the work on his defense.

There was also a contingent of Yugoslavians, including two under contract to Boston—Dino Radja and

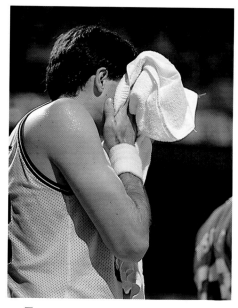

For a variety of reasons, Kevin McHale decided to show up at the Celtics' rookie camp.

7'2" Stojko Vrankovic. Over the past two seasons, both have played overseas rather than testing their skills in America. The camp offered them another opportunity to contemplate the big time.

"I think it is time for me to see if I can play in the NBA," Vrankovic told the Boston Globe's Peter May.

The camp, which opened Saturday July 21 and ran through Tuesday July 24, featured two daily sessions. In the morning, they practiced and ran through drills. At night, they scrimmaged before a packed, humid house of Celtics fans and hoops junkies.

For the fans, the camp offered a pageant of intensity. They could see

players virtually scrambling for their professional lives. Every other sequence seemed to feature some young wolf in a full extension, mindless of screeching floor burns, diving after a loose ball he had no hope of getting.

The scoreboard was lit for the scrimmages but never moved off the 00-00. It didn't have to. The only real points were to be scored in the minds of management. The coaches and scouts sat on the sideline, taking it all in.

"It's a lot of guys going 110 percent, going at each other real hard," explained Dave Popson, a veteran free agent who has literally traveled the basketball world in search of a home.

"I'm trying to make the team," he said. "Trying to impress somebody, trying to catch a scout's eye, a coach's eye, or whatever."

A big-name high-school player who never quite lived up to his reputation in college, Popson came out of the University of North Carolina in 1987 as the third pick of the Detroit Pistons. After being cut by the Pistons, he played pro ball in France. Then he returned to the Pistons the next fall and made a strong impression but still failed to make the cut. From there, he caught on with the Los Angeles Clippers, hanging on until Danny Manning returned from injury. After that, he spent time with the Albany Patroons in the CBA until the Miami Heat picked him up. He finished the 1989 season in Miami and almost became a Celtic for 1989-90. He earned an invitation to Boston's training camp but was cut just before the season opened. So he went to Spain, played for good money, and averaged 16 points and seven rebounds per game.

Eric McArthur soars.

McHale watches the camp action.

On the strength of that showing, the 6'9" Popson was again ready to make a run for the Celtics' roster. For a free agent, the toughest decision is where to put your efforts. Popson figured Boston was his best choice. "I feel comfortable playing here," he explained. "And that was a big part of my decision in trying here again. They play a good team style."

On the very first night of scrimmaging, Popson collided with another player and suffered a gash over his left eye that required three stitches. He shook it off and kept banging the rest of the session. The mental anguish in the world of free agency is much worse than the pain anyway. The toughest thing is trying to read the coaches.

"Especially when they're not talking to you," Popson said. "You sit in your room at night wondering, 'What do they think about me? What did I do? I threw that ball away too many times. I missed that shot coming down on the break.' It goes through your mind. It's just human nature."

Essential to the toughness necessary to make it as a free agent is a healthy dose of patience. If hope doesn't spring eternal, it at least has to get you through the preseason. "Sometimes you get overlooked, especially at a camp like this where there are a lot of guys," Popson said. "You might just not get your chance. It might not come. Maybe this year or next year it might come. Maybe two

years, or whatever."

"Whatever" is usually a decent contract in the hinterlands. Among the spectators was Tony Souveryns, the coach of a Belgium team. He was looking for an American power forward or center, preferably a youngster not too cynical about the game. Souveryns said he could offer about $50,000 plus an apartment and other amenities for the right young player. The money is better in other European leagues, but considering that the CBA pays less than half that, the Belgian option is an attractive safety net for those who fail to make the NBA grade.

One player who didn't get overlooked in camp was rookie free agent Eric McArthur out of the

The nightly sessions were a treat for the fans.

University of California-Santa Barbara. Armed with solid skills, an excellent attitude, and enough enthusiasm to charge a pep band, McArthur stood out among the free agents. The only negative was his height, 6'6", on the short side for an NBA forward, unless that forward happens to be Charles Barkley or Adrian Dantley. No one is ready to project McArthur as another Barkley, but Celtics radio color analyst Glen Ordway says McArthur would have been a first-round pick if he were only two inches taller.

But he doesn't seem to miss the height, at least not in this camp. During the final scrimmage Tuesday night, he was everywhere. Inside with the ball, he went with a pump fake, letting the ball roll free up through his fingers, just enough to get his defender airborne. Then he rose up for a jarring right-handed jam. Moments later he hit a smooth eight-foot jumper. And a sequence later, he pulled down a defensive rebound and headed up floor, taking the center lane and dropping off a neat bounce pass to Reggie Lewis for the score.

The crowd applauded this enthusiastically, as it did a short time later when he took off at the foul line on his way to a jam. He completed the performance by scrambling after a loose ball, retrieving it before it went out of bounds and whipping a pass downcourt for another bucket. When he left the floor for a substitution, the crowd applauded again.

All of which registered in the minds of management, particularly his enthusiasm. On a roster of quiet, conservative veterans, the Celtic brass figures they can use his spirit.

"I think that's why a guy like an Eric McArthur has a chance to make our team," Dave Gavitt said of the rookie. "We need a little bit of that."

"He's a guy who has some fire," Chris Ford agreed. "He'll have to continue to show that fire. He has the ability to be a pretty good defender. He's aggressive and bangs people. If anybody gets into tussles in training camp, he'll probably be the one."

Sure enough, the Celtics signed McArthur to a contract in September.

Popson, too, got another invitation to training camp. His gamble of coming to Boston's rookie camp had paid off.

THE TEACHER

The young players used the nighttime scrimmages to show what they could do, but the mornings were reserved for teaching and drills. It was in these sessions that McHale starred.

"He's got some of the best post moves anybody's ever had," said Red Auerbach.

The Celtics' power forward took the time to teach some of tricks to the young big men. He offered plenty of encouragement and demonstrated the do's and don'ts of playing the post in the NBA.

For example, he showed the group what might happen if a player tried to post up by merely leaning his upper body against his defender. That approach made it easier for the

The young players used the nighttime scrimmages to show what they could do, but the mornings were reserved for teaching and drills.

defender to steal the ball, or he could simply step back and let the off-balance post man fall to the floor.

It was better, McHale said, to keep the defender on your hip, to spread a bit and post up from a solid base. With your stance spread, a defender would find it much more difficult to reach around you and steal the ball, he pointed out.

McHale, the teacher, leaves Auerbach beaming. During the 1989

offseason, McHale held a minicamp for Boston's young big men—Ed Pinckney, Joe Kleine and Radja—at Auerbach's request.

"He's a super kid," the Celtics' president said of McHale. "He's got lots of patience and lots of fun."

McHale's tutoring is worth its weight in uranium because post play has become something of a lost art in basketball. But McHale knows that art and uses it nightly and can demonstrate it in his sleep.

"In college they don't teach the post that much," Auerbach says. "Maybe coaches don't know it. They evade it, hoping the big guys will pick it up."

Kleine, who virtually idolizes McHale, credits working with the Celtics' star last summer as a major reason for the improvement in his game.

"I owe a lot to him," Kleine said last spring.

Ford makes a point with the campers.

The Celtic brass is pinning their hopes on Dee Brown.

McHale's appearance at the rookie camp brought the same kind of response.

"I think he's great," Michael Smith said. "First of all, not only is he a great player, but he's a great individual. Sometimes in this league it's easy to assume that somebody is a great person just because they're a great player. That's not necessarily the case, but in this case it is. He's a great person. He thinks of others. Here he is, going into his 11th season, a perennial All-Star, All-Defensive player, All-Everything, and yet he'll fly in here, leave his family in Minnesota and come in not just to help himself, but to help the young kids. That type of attitude has to carry over to the whole team."

McHale's appearance at a rookie camp could mean good things for the coming season, Reggie Lewis said. "I think it makes a statement that Kevin is really looking forward to the season. By him coming out here he's showing he's going to be ready for it, and he's taking it real seriously."

The same, of course, could be said for Lewis himself. "We know what we have to do to get back on top," he said. "Kevin, Bagley and myself coming to camp shows that we're trying to make sure we're ready for the season."

McHale, however, shrugged off the praise and downplayed his appearance as merely an opportunity to see how his thumb was recovering after offseason surgery.

"I wanted to try out my thumb and see how it was," he said. "It gives me

a chance to play some basketball, but it's really not that big of a deal. I only came down to spend a few days. It's not like I spent a month here at rookie camp."

As far as the difficulty of dining with the wolves, McHale shrugged that off, too. "I got a little running in," he said. "It felt pretty comfortable."

Although he's a natural teacher, don't mention coaching as part of his future. "I'll never do that," he said. "Basketball is something I do for a living, and it's something I enjoy, but it's not something I want to do day in and day out. There are a lot of things in life more interesting to me than that."

He derives much joy from the game, and somehow the idea of coaching seems to detract from that.

Red has fun with the campers.

Ford not only talks, he listens.

The wolves scrap.

"You gotta have fun," he said. "Everytime I'm playing basketball I'm having fun. If I quit having fun, I'll quit playing basketball."

For the same reason, he really doesn't like looking down the road too far. "I *am* down the road in this profession," he said. "I've got a few more years left in me. I'm going to wait and see. Everybody goes through a period in their career where they play and improve. They play 'cause the money's good. I'm just at the point where I play 'cause I like to

play. It has nothing to do with money or fame or notoriety. I just play 'cause I love to play basketball. And it's a very comfortable feeling to play like this 'cause I know if I don't enjoy it any more I'm going to leave."

Obviously, in some ways the game isn't as fun as it used to be because the Celtics haven't won a title in four seasons. But on the other hand, McHale is finding subtle pleasures in his career. "When you're younger, you do a lot of things better physically and you don't have to work at it as

hard. I think that now I have more of an appreciation for the game, for the little nuances of the game."

A part of those simple pleasures is finding new ideas for his bag of tricks. "Every time I play I take something away that is new and refreshing and fun," he said, "and that's why I love it."

It's also why he doesn't mind spending a little time with the hungry young wolves.

Reggie, the bright light in Boston's future.

Young Guns

Just about every day last spring, Curtis Taylor would get the dreaded wake-up call before 6 a.m. That's when Dee Brown would get him out of bed to go shoot basketball.

Never mind that their season for the Jacksonville University was over. Never mind that it was the end of their senior year, time for having fun and taking it easy. Dee Brown wanted to work.

"Dee would be saying, 'I gotta get better,' " Taylor said, shaking his head and smiling.

So they'd truck over to the gym and blast away non-stop for nearly two hours. Afterward, just when Taylor figured he could get a shower and jump back in the rack for a little snooze before classes, Brown announced that they should run suicide sprints.

"I'd be dead tired," Taylor said, "but Dee just kept saying, 'I gotta get better.' "

The 21-year-old Brown never held summer jobs while growing up in Jacksonville. His work was basketball.

Apparently that attitude has paid off for Brown, Boston's first-round pick in last spring's draft. With the Celtics seeking to step up their intensity, his quickness and athletic ability mean that he could see a good amount of playing time as a rookie point guard this season.

The idea of playing with the Celtics' great frontcourt has left Brown feeling like a kid at Christmas. He and Taylor gave Jacksonville the best set of guards in the Sun Belt Conference over the past few seasons, but the Dolphins had no big men. When injuries further

If the Celtics are to rise to the top of the NBA again, they'll need some young guns to step forward and develop as real players.

decimated the team's frontcourt, coach Rich Haddad had to move the 6'2" Brown to forward.

After a year of playing out of position, he's eager to get back to his game.

"That's what I love about this team," Brown said of the Celtics. "They have three of the best big men in the league and then one of the best upcoming guards in Reggie Lewis. You've got everything here that you need, especially what I've been missing to really enhance my game as a point guard. I was really playing out of position in two of my four years at JU."

Improbable as it sounds, the Celtics may need his work ethic and

enthusiasm even more than his quickness in 1990-91.

Indeed, if the Celtics are to rise to the top of the NBA again, they'll need some young guns to step forward and develop as real players. It's now Chris Ford's job to make sure they do just that. He has to find those people who want to be part of the club's future.

"It's a tough transition," Ford says, "but our veteran players are still talented enough. We need some support. We need guys to fight and play as hard as they can. In recent seasons, the attitude hasn't been such."

Ford said that his predecessor, Jimmy Rodgers, fought to instill that hard-work attitude, but coaches have trouble reaching their players in the age of long-term, guaranteed contracts.

"It's tough," Boston's new coach said. "Our young players need to approach the game more like our veterans—Kevin and Larry and Robert—approach it."

As a player, Ford worked hard to develop his ability. He knows what it takes. "You have to continue to improve your game every day," he said. "There are some individuals who don't go as hard as they could. There are some guys who don't attack their games and try to improve them."

REGGIE

A noted exception, of course, is Reggie Lewis, who is well on his way to becoming a Celtics star in his own right. Rather than part of the problem, Reggie has worked to become a big part of the solution.

"We need more Reggie Lewises," says Dave Gavitt, the Celtics' new director of basketball operations.

Opponents around the NBA wouldn't mind having one themselves. "I think Reggie may be the most underrated player in the league," Knicks coach Stu Jackson said last season. "He does what you're supposed to do. He puts the ball in the basket. Because the Celtics are so great, you tend to forget about him and he kills you."

The team's first round pick in 1987, the 24-year-old Lewis has done

> **"I think Reggie may be the most underrated player in the league."**
>
> **—New York Knicks coach Stu Jackson**

everything asked of him in Boston. He waited his turn and learned from the bench during his first season. A natural small forward at 6'7", Reggie filled that role nicely during Bird's absence in 1988-89. Then he shifted to big guard as a starter last year, because that's where the Celtics needed him.

To prepare for the shift, he spent the summer of 1989 working on his ballhandling. The summer of 1990 found him back at that same grind, playing full-court one-on-one with smaller, quicker players back in his native Baltimore.

"I've just been working out with a lot of guys that are quicker than me," he said over the offseason. "I think that's been helping me out a great deal."

His biggest adjustment as a guard has been keeping lower to the floor. "That's my biggest problem, keeping my back bent," he said. "Once I get used to having my back bent, I'll be okay."

Most observers feel he passed okay a long ways back and is well on his way to excellent. Lewis admits to seeing improvement last season, part

Dee-lighted to be a Celtic.

of which was attributable to his ability to mix patience with steady work. "As last year progressed, I started to get more relaxed with my ballhandling," he said. "It's just something that takes time. The more comfortable I get, the better my ballhandling skills will be."

He also spent time working on his outside shooting during the offseason. "I think I'll shoot more threes this year," he said. To that end, he lifted high repetitions of light weights to add strength and increase the range on his shots. And for style,

he added a goatee. "Just a little something I grew over the summer," he explained. "But I think I'll keep it."

Ford hopes the other younger players will take note of Reggie's example. The more he has improved, the more the Celtics have improved.

As an added touch, Reggie came to the Celtics rookie camp in July. "I let the coaches and the owners know that I am ready to go this year," he said.

Despite his personal progress, last season brought a round of disappointments. The Celtics lost in the first round of the playoffs, which led to the dismissal of Jimmy Rodgers. "Jimmy is a great guy," Reggie said, "and I really enjoyed playing for him and working with him. I was sad to see him go. But Chris is the head coach now, and I think he's going to do an excellent job. He's a great guy also, and I enjoy working with him, too. He knows the system, and he can relate to all the players. He played with most of the guys. It's fun being around Chris. He makes the game fun."

As a former player, Ford should be able to get more out of the veterans, Lewis said. "I think all the guys respect him and will work hard to please Chris."

FIRE

Over the past few seasons, the Celtics have lacked a fiery, emotional leader. The team's veterans are all the types who prefer to lead quietly, by the example of their play, which has left Ford looking for a player with more emotion.

"Reggie is in the same mold as our veteran players," Ford said. "He's very quiet on the floor. It's tough when you don't have enough of a mix of players, when everybody is quiet and even-tempered. You need guys who are gonna be feisty out there. It could lead to being a passive team. And we have been a passive team the last couple of years."

The one player on the roster who has showed that fire is backup center Joe Kleine. Ford looks for Joe to provide more of the same, but the team needs even more emotion.

Rookie/ free agent Eric McArthur out of the University of California-Santa Barbara could provide some of that fire, Ford said. And so could Brian Shaw, who finally agreed to return to the Celtics after spending a year playing in Italy for Il Messaggero.

PINCKNEY

With Shaw, Brown and Lewis forming a solid nucleus of guards,

Smith spent the summer working on his game.

Ford hopes to get more production out of reserve forward Ed Pinckney, who began last season as a starter before seeing his playing time tail off as the schedule progressed.

In all fairness to Pinckney, the Celtics haven't had the guards to take advantage of his ability to run the floor, Ford said. "He will excel with guards who push it up the floor. I'd like to see Ed Pinckney get some fire in him. He's a guy who's got very good skills."

The coach, however, wants Pinckney to can his laid-back demeanor.

"We're getting rid of that 'Easy Ed' nickname," Ford said. "There's no Easy Ed any more."

After being traded twice in his young pro career, then losing his starting job in Boston, Pinckney's confidence seemed to plummet. The coaches will do what they can to restore it, Ford said. They badly want Pinckney, the Most Outstanding Player of the 1985 Final Four, to regain his spirit.

"But he has to want it," Ford said. "He has to play with emotion and get fired up."

Kleine needs help firing up the team.

MICHAEL SMITH

Another question mark is the 1989 first-round draft pick, Michael Smith, a 6'10" forward. Smith is a gifted offensive player, but he reported to camp out of shape last year and struggled to catch up. He finally showed his form on a western road trip and proved he was a legitimate offensive threat.

Now he needs to show Ford that he can play at the other end of the floor.

"Michael really has to improve his defense," the coach said frankly. "With the athletes out there today, it's tough to stop someone cold. But if you keep breaking down individually, guys go by you for easy buckets."

Smith needs to work on keeping his man in front and directing him to an area of the floor where there is defensive help, Ford said.

Until that happens, it will be difficult for the Celtics' coaches to give him any great amount of playing time.

The good news is that Smith is determined not to find himself behind again this season. He came to rookie camp to work on his defense and went to Los Angeles as part of Boston's entry in the rookie league.

With that kind of continued effort, Smith could improve enough defensively to start helping the team, Ford said.

DEE BROWN

Dee Brown first started fooling with computers when he was 10 years old.

"My family is math-oriented, computer-oriented," he explained.

The Celtics, of course, are eager to see if he can bring computer-like decisions to the task of point guard when he runs Boston's fastbreak.

Detroit General Manager Jack McCloskey said the Pistons had their hearts set on drafting Brown in the first round, but Boston got him first. The Pistons' scouting staff had Brown rated very high in competitiveness. In addition to his basketball skills, Brown is smart, McCloskey said.

"It's just something that I take pride in," Brown said when asked about his competitiveness. "When you're playing basketball, it's like any other

"Easy Ed" no more.

Bagley (left) and Smith (right) will fight for roster spots.

challenge in life. You've got to play hard and be competitive if you want to be the best. I've always been told I wasn't big enough, so I've had to play extra hard, be extra tough."

Brown has no problem figuring his biggest adjustment ahead in Boston.

"The 82-game schedule," he said. "If you go all the way to the Finals, it's like 115 games, and that's a whole four-year career in college. They told me that it's grueling, that you have to have the right diet, or you'll hit the wall around 40 games because you're not used to it."

For Brown, one of the treats of being a Celtic is getting to talk to Red Auerbach. "He likes to see you work out and stuff," Brown said. "We talk about things he wants me to do as a point guard. He says a lot of funny things. He's a very intelligent person; he's got a sense of humor, but he is also serious when he talks to me about basketball. He's very serious about that."

Because he had to play out of position at Jacksonville, Brown hasn't played the point much over the past year. But he's not worried about being rusty. "You don't forget how to play point guard," he said. "You're a point guard by nature."

The best part about the position is the decision-making it requires, Brown said. "I like having control. I like to be the kind of point guard that doesn't have to pound the ball in the ground. I'm a player that doesn't need the ball to make things happen."

The idea of coming in and playing immediately in Boston has his competitive juices flowing. "You know," he said, "not many rookie point guards come in and run a championship-caliber basketball team. Tim Hardaway did a good job last year with Golden State, but they finished under .500. If you've got players around you like this, you just do what you know and you're going to be in good shape."

Ford says there is an oft-repeated observation about rookies in the NBA. They show immediately whether they're ready to play or not. The Celtics need help this season, and they'll have to find out quickly if Brown is ready.

This fall will be the time when he findsout if all those early-morning shooting sessions have paid off.

"I'm real relaxed about it," Brown said. "You have to go through life that way. You can't be tense about too many things. You only go around once. I try to make the most out of everything I do the first time around."

That, of course, is just what Ford wants to hear. The Celtics need some young guns to step forward and play with the veterans. If that happens, this team just might exceed expectations.

And that's always a tough thing to do in Boston.

There's no harder-working Celtic than Parish.

Red has his memories.

Auerbach: The Ornery Winner

The 1990-91 NBA season will mark the 25th anniversary of Red Auerbach's retirement from coaching. As opponents around the league will attest, he's still a pretty fiery guy. But some things have changed for the 74-year-old redhead. For one thing, he suffers dumb questions from writers a little better than he used to.

A writer recently asked him if he was aware that the silver anniversary of his retirement was coming up.

"Yep," he said.

Did he miss coaching? the writer asked.

"Oh sure," he said, "you miss it a lot. You can't do something for 20 years at a professional level and not miss it."

Auerbach retired following the 1965-66 season, after his team had won its eighth straight (and ninth overall) NBA World Championship. The Celtics went on to win two more championships over the next three seasons. Regardless, Auerbach said he had no regrets about stepping down when he did.

"I had to make a choice," he explained. "Either I got into management then, when it had to be done, or wait four or five years and then look around and see. Everything is a matter of timing."

The timing in this case concerned the club's general managership. Long-time team owner Walter Brown had died in 1964, leaving Auerbach to fill the dual role of coach and general manager for two seasons. That task left him exhausted. He once

As opponents around the league will attest, he's still a pretty fiery guy. But some things have changed for the 74-year-old redhead.

explained to good friend Lefty Driesell that the mere act of putting on his sneakers to go to practice had become drudgery. At the end of the 1965 season, he knew he either had to find a coach or a general manager.

Having gotten his fill of the bench, Auerbach decided to coach one more season while he looked around for a successor. Once that was done, he would become a full-time general manager.

Without tremendous fanfare, Auerbach closed the chapter on the most successful coaching career in the history of professional sports. In his 20 seasons of coaching, he won a league-record 938 regular-season games. It is a record that has never been broken, although Auerbach thinks it eventually will.

"It will be broken in time if guys can last that long mentally," he said. "Because I did it in 20 years; I don't know whether a lot of guys will do it in 20 years."

An immensely proud man, Auerbach says he takes the most pride in the consistency of winning that the record represents. He also takes pride in the fact that the Celtics accomplished their championships with meager team resources. Brown, after all, had funded the team out of his own pocket for years, which meant that the entire Celtics organization consisted of four people. Auerbach had no assistant coaches. He did his own scouting and managed the team's business affairs, right down to booking plane flights and hotel rooms.

"We had no money to speak of," he said. "We were still in the process of selling the game to the Boston area."

Slowly the fans began appreciating the Celtics' winning ways, but that still didn't translate into overwhelming cash flow. Whereas a wealthy team like the New York Knicks could afford to buy players, Auerbach spent his time shopping for bargains, either unheralded rookies or supposedly

Heinsohn scores against the Hawks in the 1961 Finals.

washed-up has-beens.

"We kept winning with mirrors, adding a player here, a player there," he said. "We did a lot of developing and teaching."

Auerbach also did a lot of motivating. The team's competitiveness was often driven by his temper. There is no better example of this than Game Three of the 1957 NBA Finals against the St. Louis Hawks, as the Celtics were on their way to their first championship. The St. Louis crowd in Kiel Auditorium had its rough edges, which included a reputation for racial and ant-Semitic epithets. Auerbach stirred this cauldron during pre-game warmups when he complained that one of the goals was too low. "I knew it was too low when Sharman and Cousy told me they could touch the rim," he explained. Auerbach took his complaint to the officials, who agreed to check the height. They found no problem. Hawks owner Ben Kerner, though, had become overheated by the delay and stalked out onto the floor to scream that Auerbach was embarrassing him in front of the home fans.

Auerbach promptly ended the tirade with a shot to Kerner's mouth. "I was talking to the refs," Auerbach later explained, "and he interrupted me."

The officials chose not to throw him out, he said, because the incident occurred before the game. The blow brought blood but no permanent damage to Kerner, who remained Red's friend long after the incident.

"When I retired he gave me wonderful gifts," Auerbach recalled.

THE PRIDE

After beating the Minneapolis Lakers 4-0 in 1959 for their second title, the Celtics emerged full-blown in the early 1960s. Bill Russell and Tommy Heinsohn were in their prime. Sam Jones moved in as a starter and a scorer to replace guard Bill Sharman, who retired in 1962. And while the careers of Bob Cousy and Frank Ramsey were winding down, Auerbach always seemed to have the right answer to keep the transition of right answer to keep the transition of talent flowing smoothly.

K.C. Jones was gaining experience as a backup to Cousy, and in 1962, the Celtics drafted John Havlicek, a good athlete but no superstar, out of Ohio State. Who could have seen that he would evolve into such a player? In retrospect, the development of the Boston dynasty was something to behold.

The Celtics beat the Hawks for the championship in 1960 and '61, and then defeated the new Los Angeles Lakers in 1962 to bring their title count to four straight. Still, many observers figured their day was over.

"The Boston Celtics are an old team," *Sports Illustrated* declared in March of 1963. "Tired blood courses through their varicose veins."

The Celtics, of course, would win their sixth title that spring and five more over the next six seasons. But *SI*'s underestimation of Boston's strength still had some basis in fact. It seemed that each February of his career Cousy had blasted the NBA for seasons that were too long. Finally weary, Cousy announced that he would retire after the 1962-63 season. Observers saw his leaving as a major loss to the Celtics. And they didn't see the wheels of Auerbach's cunning turning.

The reason for this was Havlicek. Auerbach had never seen Havlicek play when he drafted him in 1962. Then in camp that summer he got his first look. "I remember I was stunned," Auerbach later told reporters. "All I could think of was, 'Ohh. Have I got something here? Are they going to think I'm smart.'"

But Havlicek was just one of several changing faces in the team's evolution. Later Auerbach would get Don Nelson and Bailey Howell and several more key pieces to the puzzle. Plus, Cousy's leaving meant the Jones duo of K.C. and Sam would become a larger factor. Most important, though, the Celtics had Bill Russell, whom former Lakers coach Fred Schaus called "the most dominant individual who ever played a team sport."

Built around this incredible player,

Red, the living legend.

the team's changes were made without problem. The coach and center had come to lord over the NBA, and it didn't make them popular. "At first I didn't like Red Auerbach," a rival NBA coach once said. "But in time I grew to hate him."

Those emotions have lasted for decades.

"Red was hated around the league," former NBA player and Hawks coach Paul Seymour said in 1990. "He wasn't a very well-liked guy. He always had the talent. He was always shooting his mouth off. If you walked up to him in the old days, he was more than likely to tell you to get lost."

Having a great player like Russell

made Auerbach a coach, said former Syracuse coach Al Cervi. "He's the biggest phony who ever walked the streets of America."

Auerbach was an early master at working the refs and officials. His footstomping and tirades, usually punctuated by a lit cigar at the end of the game, had begun to wear on his opponents by the mid-1960s. Plus, the NBA was getting more television exposure, and his antics weren't always pleasant to view.

"Red was a very astute judge of talent," said Schaus, whose Laker teams battled Auerbach's Celtics four times in the Finals. "When you have a lot of stars, you have to keep them happy and playing as a team. Red did

Boston battled the Lakers in the '60s. (Photo by Jerry Buckley)

that. I didn't like some of the things he did and said when I competed against him. Some of the things he said would bother me. But the guy who wore No. 6 out there bothered us more. You had to change your game completely because of Russell."

But for Lakers star Jerry West, Auerbach on the sidelines was more entertainment than irritation. "Red was outspoken," West said. "His sideline antics were funny. I happened to like him very much. When you talk to his ex-players, they all have great respect for him. I don't know how many players feel that way about their former coaches."

Some coaches didn't have Auerbach's success because they didn't have his timing. They tried to intimidate the officials throughout the game, Auerbach said. "You work the refs only when you feel you're right. You had to pick your spots. Sure I was active. You had to be active. But it wasn't all the time."

As for the enmity from other coaches that still burned nearly three decades later, Auerbach said, "Any time you're winning, you get criticism. Nothing instigates jealousy like winning. When you're winning, they find a thousand reasons to take potshots. You don't pay attention. You just keep doing what you're doing."

This debate over Auerbach flared regularly over the winter and spring of 1963. His relationship with official Sid Borgia carried a particular spite. The Boston press took to calling Borgia "Big Poison."

"I'm convinced," Auerbach said after one game, "that it would be the highlight of his career if he refereed the game in which we lost the championship. He doesn't like me, he doesn't like Cousy and he doesn't like the Celtics."

Whether he really wanted it or not, Borgia would never get that opportunity. The aged Celtics beat the Lakers in 1963 for their sixth title. "Please," Auerbach crowed to the press, "tell me some of these stories about Los Angeles being the basketball capital of the world."

"It's nice to be playing with the old

By 1964, Red had won seven championships and had never been named coach of the year. Still, he pushed on with his singular style.

pros," Russell said. "The old, old pros."

There was no champagne or beer in the Boston locker room. Why celebrate? replied Heinsohn when asked about it. "We've won five in a row."

The 1963-64 season brought Auerbach another series of crafty personnel moves to crow about—the addition of veteran center Clyde Lovellette and 6'6" Willie Naulls in the frontcourt. Naulls would provide double-figure scoring as a key substitute for three important years, and Lovellette gave them some good

games, too. Auerbach also added Larry Siegfried, Havlicek's teammate out of Ohio State who would mature into a double-figures scorer in a few seasons.

The big change for 1963-64 came with the league's balance of power. Maurice Podoloff had retired as commissioner and was replaced by Walter Kennedy. In an even bigger move, the Warriors had left Philadelphia to move to San Francisco, where they took charge in the Western Conference with what appeared to be one of the most powerful teams in NBA history.

But that was on paper, Auerbach pointed out. "I've seen a lot of great teams, at least on paper, that won nothing."

Warriors coach Alex Hannum called it his "muscle and hustle team."

Wilt Chamberlain was the chief muscle. But there was plenty more. There was 6'11", 230-pound Nate Thurmond, a rookie out of Bowling Green who had yet to develop offensively. Then there were 6'8"

Havlicek was a prized find out of Ohio State.

As player and coach, Russell battled Wilt.

A cigar and a smile.

Wayne Hightower, a fine shooter, and 6'6", 215-pound Tom Meschery, who helped in the muscle department. The crafty backcourt included Al Attles, Guy Rodgers and Gary Phillips.

"That was a powerful, physical team," Auerbach said. "Chamberlain and Thurmond were two of the best centers in the game."

But the Warriors were no match for Boston in the big show. Frank Ramsey, all of 6'3", psyched out Thurmond on defense, and the Celtics waltzed to the lead. Chamberlain was a power, but Russell forced him into taking a fallaway jumper. In one sequence in Game One, a 108-96 Boston win, Russell blocked Wilt's shot, only to see Thurmond get the loose ball and take it back up. Russell blocked that one, too.

"He never stops throwing you something new," an impressed Rodgers said of Russell afterward.

The Celtics took the series, 4-1, for their sixth consecutive championship. "A lot of teams have come and gone since we first beat St. Louis in '57," Ramsey told reporters.

Auerbach had won seven championships and had never been named coach of the year. Still, he pushed on with his singular style.

During the season, he had fined several players for a transgression of team rules. They asked him to reconsider. "Get lost," he replied, "if you don't know by now that the Celtics are a dictatorship. I am a dictator and it's about time you found out."

Asked about his style, he told reporters: "Look, I don't worry about handling them. I worry about how they handle me. I'm not here as a doormat. Let them adjust to me. Anybody who comes to this team better take a little time to figure out what I'm like and learn to please me."

Despite his gruffness, he had a real flair for sales, and even represented several products on the side. "Selling keeps me alert during the season," he explained. "I meet clients when I'm on the road."

With this seventh title, it began to appear as if Boston might never lose. Auerbach projected that much. "The thrill never goes from winning," he said. "But maybe the reasons change. First, it was just trying to win a title. Now it is a question of going down as the greatest team of all time. That stimulates you."

The closing of the '64 season brought the retirement of Jim Loscutoff and Ramsey. Loscutoff had once sworn that as soon as he turned in his uniform he was going to belt Auerbach. Using the psychology he was known for, the coach had determined that he couldn't criticize Cousy, Ramsey or Russell. They just couldn't or wouldn't take it. So he had used Heinsohn or Loscutoff to tonguelash when he needed to communicate displeasure with the team's play.

But Loscutoff's plan was never realized. Like the rest of the Celtics, he said he loved Auerbach more than he hated him. The coach had an ability to be close and detached at the same time.

"His whole theory behind basketball is never get too close to the players' wives," Loscutoff said.

He couldn't make good coaching decisions if he knew a player's family well, Auerbach explained. "You can't be emotionally involved and impartial at the same time."

THE BURDEN

Walter Brown died in August 1964, leaving Auerbach alone to guide the Celtics on to greatness. Brown's passing and the fact that a new group of young officials had come into the league convinced the Boston coach to tone down his act somewhat.

He still prowled the sidelines while clutching a tightly rolled game program. And he still picked his spots. He just didn't pick them as often or as loudly. It some ways it didn't matter. Every time he stirred from the bench during a road game, the boos followed him.

In the spring of 1965, he appeared on a television talk show and seemed startled when the audience clapped politely. "How come they applauded?" Auerbach asked the host. "It makes me feel uneasy."

Still, he conceded his image had changed. Going into the 1965 playoffs, he had been fined less than $1,000 by the league, an unusually low figure for him. By no means was he squeaky clean, though.

"If you get obnoxious, you get incentive," he told his players.

He regularly offered young coaches tips on how to get ahead— place the scorer's and timer's table near your bench at home, and when you're on the road, wait until the other team has taken the floor for warm-ups to request their basket. Anything that disconcerted the opponent was viewed as an asset.

While he talked these precepts, he employed them less and less as he neared the end of his coaching

Sam Jones, perpetrator of the bank shot.

career. Red had mellowed, the writers covering the Celtics concluded.

Still, there were some things in his act that he refused to tone down. League officials had sent him notes saying that it didn't look good for him to light cigars on the bench.

Auerbach told the league he would stop his cigars when other coaches stopped their cigarettes, a response that angered some of his colleagues in the profession. A few coaches complained that Auerbach had an endorsement with Blackstone, a cigar company, and that he was putting on "an act."

"If this was an act, I'd be an actor," he replied. "I wouldn't be a coach."

Boy, could he coach. The Celtics broke their own record for regular-season wins in 1964-65 with 62. And Auerbach finally got his coach-of-the-year award.

"He's getting the maximum out of me," Russell told reporters.

They added their eighth championship that year, but things in the Eastern Division became complicated at mid-season when San Francisco traded Chamberlain back to the new Philadelphia 76ers (the old Syracuse Nationals). Boston had finished well atop the standings but had to fight Philly in the playoffs through another seven-game series. Chamberlain's team wasn't vanquished until Havlicek stole an in-bounds pass under Philadelphia's basket with five seconds remaining,

Coaching and winning wore Red down. (Photo courtesy of the Boston Celtics)

Auerbach mellowed toward the close of his coaching career.

which, of course, led to Johnny Most's famous line, "Havlicek stole the ball!!!"

For the record, Havlicek deflected the ball to Sam Jones, who raced downcourt to celebrate.

With the momentum from that drama, the Celtics went on to meet the Lakers in the Finals once again. Los Angeles, though, had been traumatized April 3 in the first game of the Western Division finals against the Baltimore Bullets when Elgin Baylor suffered a severe knee injury.

"I went up for a shot and my knee exploded," Baylor recalled. "I could hear a crack and a pop and everything else."

"That was really tragic," West said of the injury, "because he was a great, great player."

West and LaRusso were left alone to lead Los Angeles. They got help from their teammates, most of whom were new, but it was impossible to replace Baylor. The Celtics, though, waltzed through Game One in Boston, 142-110, as K.C. Jones held West to 26 points. "K.C. Jones used to tackle West rather than let him get off a jump shot," Schaus said.

Reporters gathered around Jones in the locker room afterward and asked him about the defensive job he had done on West. Jones made the mistake of talking.

West got 45 in Game Two, but Boston still controlled the outcome, 129-123. Wounded as they were, the Lakers managed a home win in Game 3, 126-105, as West hit for 43. The Los Angeles crowd celebrated by pelting Auerbach with cigars. Game

Red with commissioner David Stern and Alan Cohen.

Four, though, was another Celtics win, 112-99, as Sam Jones scored 37. They went back to Boston to end it, 129-96, as the Celtics outscored the Lakers 72-48 in the second half. At the outset of the fourth period, Boston ran off 20 unanswered points, while the Lakers went scoreless for five minutes. In one stretch, West missed 14 out of 15 shots. They kept hitting the back of the rim. Russell played despite an eye injury and had 30 rebounds.

After the playoffs, Auerbach announced that he would coach one more season, then retire to the front office. He explained privately that coaching had become a burden. Perhaps more than any NBA coach ever, he loved winning, but success had taken its toll. He was nearing 50 and feeling 70. With Walter Brown's death, the administrative load was heavier. Auerbach could no longer do both jobs.

Reporters asked Auerbach what the highlights of his coaching days had been. "After 1,500 games, who could remember?" he replied. "What you remember is how hard it was to get each individual win."

The wins got even harder in that final season of 1965-66. The Eastern Division was a dogfight. Chamberlain and the 76ers took some of the starch out of the Boston dynasty. Heinsohn had retired at the end of the previous season, and Havlicek became a starter. Don Nelson, acquired after Los Angeles released him, inherited the role of sixth man. For the first time in a decade, the Celtics didn't win the Eastern Division title. The 76ers won 55 games and Boston 54. But Boston regrouped in the playoffs. Philly had received a first-round bye, while Boston fended off Cincinnati in a preliminary round. The layoff hurt Chamberlain and the Sixers. They were caught flat in the Eastern finals

as Boston won, 4-1. Boston had lost six of 10 games to Philadelphia during the season, but again it was Russell's team that went on to play for the title.

The 1966 championship series quickly turned into another Celtics/Lakers scrap. Baylor had returned from knee injury, and Los Angeles had regained its potency. The Celtics had a 38-20 lead in Game One in the Garden, but the Lakers fought back to tie it late. With the score even in the final minute, Russell blocked a Baylor shot and was called for goaltending. Sam Jones scored for Boston to send it to overtime, where Baylor and West propelled the Lakers to a win, 133-129, for a 1-0 lead. Baylor had scored 36, West 41. But instead of the glory and the psychological edge falling to the Lakers, the attention abruptly shifted to Boston. Auerbach picked the postgame interview session to announce that Russell would be his replacement as head coach. For months the speculation had been that Cousy, then the coach at Boston College, would get the job. Working as a player-coach, Boston's center would become the first black head coach in a major American sport. Auerbach had talked briefly with Cousy and Heinsohn about taking the job, but both men agreed no one could better motivate Russell than Russell himself.

The announcement made headlines the next morning, while the Lakers' major victory was almost obscured, a fact that leaves Auerbach gleeful to this day.

With the future of the team settled, the Celtics bore down on the Lakers, winning the second game in the Garden, 129-109, then adding two more victories in Los Angeles for a 3-1 lead. The major problem for the Lakers was Havlicek, who could swing between guard and forward. Schaus had tried to play Rudy LaRusso, a forward, on Havlicek, but it hadn't worked.

"No one in the league his size is even close to Havlicek in quickness," Schaus told reporters.

So the Lakers coach put LaRusso on the pine and played guard Gail Goodrich on Havlicek. West moved to forward, and this three-guard lineup left Los Angeles weak on the boards. But it worked for a time. West, Baylor and Goodrich lashed back and won Games Five and Six to tie the series at three apiece.

Game Seven in the Garden was another classic. The Celtics took a big lead, as Baylor and West were a combined 3 for 18 from the floor in the first half. But as usual, the Lakers came back, cutting the Boston lead to six with 20 seconds left. Still, it seemed time for Red to light another victory cigar. The Lakers took fire with that, cutting the lead to two, 95-93, with four seconds left. Just as they had for years, the fans rushed the floor to celebrate a Boston championship. But the '66 celebration was premature and out-of-hand. Russell, who had played with a broken bone in his foot and had still gotten 32 rebounds, was knocked

Red had his cake and ate it , too.

down. Orange juice containers on the Boston bench were spilled across the floor, and Celtic Satch Sanders lost his shirt to the crowd. Somehow, K.C. Jones got the inbounds pass to Havlicek, who dribbled out the clock for championship number nine, 95-93.

Schaus said later that he would love to have been able to shove the victory cigar down Auerbach's throat. "We came awfully close to putting that damn thing out," the Lakers coach said.

At Auerbach's retirement dinner, Russell addressed the gathering: "When I took this job, somebody said, 'What did you take it for? You have nothing to gain. You've got to follow Red Auerbach.'

"I don't think I'm going to be

another Red Auerbach," Russell continued, then turned to his former coach. "Personally, I think you're the greatest basketball coach that ever lived. You know, over the years... I heard a lot of coaches and writers say the only thing that made you a great coach was Bill Russell. It helped. But that's not what did it.

"Now this is kind of embarrassing, but I'll go so far, Red, as to say this: I like you. And I'll admit there aren't very many men that I like. But you I do. For a number of reasons. First of all, I've always been able to respect you. I don't think you're a genius, just an extraordinarily intelligent man. We'll be friends until one of us dies. And I don't want too many friends, Red."

The Volk View

The 1990-91 season will be Jan Volk's seventh as general manager of the Boston Celtics. His tenure with the team began in 1971 after his graduation from law school. Over the years, he has worked in just about every aspect of team operations.

"Jan Volk is the best when it comes to the legal and contractual considerations of an NBA franchise," said Los Angeles Lakers General Manager Jerry West. "He's the best in the league."

Volk, Red Auerbach and Dave Gavitt (Boston's new head of basketball operations) comprise a formidable management triumvirate.

Volk admits that they have a challenge ahead of them, working against the salary cap to maintain Boston's excellence. The difficulty, Volk says, is making the transition to a younger team while remaining competitive. To that end, the Celtics continue to acquire and develop young players, all the while keeping intact the core of veteran stars.

Q: You like to have firmly established goals heading into a season. What's at the top of Boston's list of priorities for 1990-91?

A: One thing we didn't do last year was to maintain a home-court dominance. In the past, the Celtics have been distinguished competitively by our virtual invincibility in the Garden. Last season, we had a pretty good road record, among the elite in the league. But our home record was not consistent with what we have come to expect from Celtic teams of the past. I would like to see us re-establish that dominance right away. When we come home, we should know we're going to win. And opposing teams coming into the Garden should have something to worry about. That's a very specific goal we want to establish right from the start.

Q: Dave Gavitt has been hired to run Boston's basketball operations. His presence would seem to give the Celtics a complete management format. You have solid experience in the legal and business side of pro basketball operations. You have Red, with his vast experience. And now you have Dave Gavitt, the brightest innovator in the history of college basketball.

A: I think Dave has so much to offer to this organization. I'm glad to have Dave on board and to be able to work with him. He's exceptionally talented in many ways. And the inclusion of him in our management team can only bring good things.

Q: Could you characterize the past year as your toughest in this job? First, you've had Larry Bird recovering from heel surgery. Then there was the legal fight over Brian Shaw's contract. With all that came the team's troubles against New York in the playoffs and the dismissal of Jimmy Rodgers.

A: It's been a tough year. But when you're immersed in things and you're dealing with problems on an ongoing basis, you very rarely reflect on the circumstances. But it has been as difficult a year as we've had. I must say, however, that the sky has brightened. Brian Shaw has rejoined the team, and Dee Brown is a promising addition. Their presence adds tremendous depth to our backcourt.

Q: You're very close to Jimmy Rodgers. Has that coaching change been one of the toughest things you've had to do?

A: Yes. It was a situation that we all found very regrettable. We would have liked for the season to end on a more positive note, with a better feeling about ourselves and what we had accomplished. Unfortunately that didn't happen, and it was best to make the change.

Q: The Celtics have been restricted by the salary cap as much as any team in the league the last few seasons. And the salary cap has now stretched again. Do you anticipate that bringing some much-needed relief in your ability to acquire new players?

A: No. That won't have any effect on us at all because we are well over the cap. We're definitely strapped. Last year at this time we did have room, and we used it effectively to sign Michael Smith and Dino Radja and to trade for John Bagley. The situation forces us to continue to develop unheralded players and free agents.

Q: Dave Gavitt said what you really needed was another Reggie Lewis.

A: If you find one, let me know. Developing other complimentary players is going to be the key to our success.

Q: The Shaw case seemed to create an international incident, at least in terms of basketball diplomacy. Are there long-term hard feelings? First, Il Messaggero, the Italian team owned by a wealthy corporation, signed Shaw away from the Celtics. He played a year in Italy, then signed to return to Boston, but Il Messaggero still attempted to lure him back for yet a second year. When the Celtics defended their rights to Shaw in court, Il Messaggero then went after Boston's newest top draft pick, Dee Brown. Fortunately, Brown told the Italians he wasn't interested. But Il Messaggero seemed to carry some vindictiveness. Are the Celtics in a feud with Il Messaggero?

A: It's hard to characterize this as anything more than an isolated situation. At least, that's what I think it is. I haven't yet been able to figure out exactly what the motivational factors are behind all of it. I hope it's not something that suggests a long-standing, tit-for-tat situation.

Q: Does this competition for the rights to Shaw suggest a trend developing?

A: There are some concerns about the impact of European basketball on the contractual stability of the NBA. As an NBA team, we have a salary cap that we have voluntarily entered into, but it becomes meaningless if you find yourself suddenly competing with teams outside the NBA that do not have the same constraints. And that's a very difficult situation.

The only thing that keeps it in check to a certain degree is the self-imposed rule in Europe that they only have two foreign players on their rosters.

Q: But if each European team has only two American players, then it has more money to spend on those two players. That would seem to give them a competitive advantage in buying high-priced Americans, because the rest of their players are lower-paid Europeans.

A: That, in fact, can be the case. What's more, the corporate sponsors of those European teams are apparently seeking American players as an advertising/ public relations ploy. They aren't basing their player contracts on the team's income. Accordingly, they can afford to overlook strict economic factors, such as attendance and television revenue. If a large corporate conglomerate owns a basketball team, it doesn't really worry about that team making money. In some cases teams find that their sponsors are willing to pay exorbitant amounts of money for a player. They do this, even though the European leagues often play far fewer games than we do. They don't have to worry much about the revenues for the team, because the team exists simply to keep the corporate sponsor's name prominent in the marketplace.

Jan Volk says the salary cap becomes meaningless if NBA teams are forced to compete with European teams that don't recognize the cap.

Q: Do you think this situation could hinder the friendly climate in international basketball?

A: I can't say it won't be repeated. Right now there is a very small group of teams that have the money to buy the best American players. We also bid on the services of their best players, so it should work out to a fair cultural exchange.

Q: What do you see in the future for the NBA's health? Will the league continue to grow?

A: I think the NBA is solid and very stable. The sport has matured.

Our fans have literally grown up with the league, playing and watching NBA basketball, knowing its history and teams. I think the product is as good as it has ever been. I think it will continue to prosper. I don't think it will continue to grow at the same rate. It's been growing at an exceptionally fast and impressive rate. But it will continue to be very popular.

Q: Having enjoyed its success, does that create additional pressure for the league to grow, and if so, is that pressure good?

A: I think any time you're in a business or industry that has shown growth over a period of time those pressures exist. You make those comparisons to the previous growth rate, and you try to keep yourself growing in a way that exceeds the preceeding year. But it's very hard, and you have to be realistic and realize that there is a time when that growth rate will slow down. Still, as long as the NBA can keep on the rise and remain a popular sport, it will grow. I think we've done a good job.

Q: Some people have said that expansion has diluted the talent too much. I know you had felt there was plenty of talent for expansion. Are you in favor of halting expansion, or do you foresee a time over the next decade when there will be 28 or 29 or 30 teams?

A: We're just at the start of the decade, and I can't predict too far out. I think we've seen the last of expansion for a number of years. As I said at the time, whenever you expand you're going to flatten out for a short period. But eventually you'll move forward. And I think the expansion teams have become more competitive each year, although they don't necessarily win a lot of ball games. But they have been exciting teams to watch. The talent level has been augmented by the draft over the last couple of years, and that will continue. Over the next couple of seasons, I think you'll see expansion teams start winning more games.

CELTICS

PROFILES

JOHN BAGLEY

Birthdate: April 23, 1960
Birthplace: Bridgeport, CT
High School: Warren Harding High (CT)
College: Boston College '83
Height: 6-0
Weight: 192
Position: Guard
Years Pro: 8 Years

How Acquired: Traded by New Jersey to Boston for 1991 and 1993 second-round draft choices on October 5, 1989.

1989-90 Season: Chosen the starting point guard before the season began... on opening night vs. Milwaukee, he registered his lone double-double of the season with 13 points and 16 assists... had 10 assists in the next game, at Chicago... started 17 times: 11/3-11/7, 11/14-11/21, 2/2-2/14, and the last three regular season games... 10+ mins 52 times... 20+ mins 23 times... 30+ mins 9 times... 10+ assts 6 times... 10+ pts 7 times... one double-double... suffered a separated left shoulder in Indiana on 11/21... put on the injured list on 11/24... activated on 1/6... returned to action on 1/12... dressed in the last five games of the eight game road trip, but did not play due to a right hamstring strain suffered in Portland on 2/16... returned vs. Dallas on 2/28... DNP-CD 6 times... played in all five games during the playoffs.

Professional Career: Drafted by Cleveland on the first-round of the 1982 draft as an undergraduate, the 12th pick overall... in his third NBA season, he accomplished a career best 35 points on February 4, 1985... finished fourth among assists leaders in 1985-86, averaging a team record 9.4 per game... traded by Cleveland (with Keith Lee) to New Jersey for Darryl Dawkins and James Bailey on October 8, 1987... in only five seasons with the Cavaliers, he became their all-time assists leader with 2,311... passed the 5,000 career scoring mark in 1988-89 and surpassed the 3,000 career assists total in the same season... in 1988-89, he started the first 20 games; later in the season, he spent 13 games on the injured list with a sprained left ankle.

College Career: Passed up his final year of eligibility to enter the NBA draft... a three-year starter at Boston College, he led the team in scoring each season... finished fourth on the all-time BC scoring list... named Big East Player of the Year for the 1980-81 campaign... set Big East records for most points (30) and most free throws (16) in one game (January 16, 1981 vs. Villanova)... ppg increased in each season, career average was 17.9.

Personal: John Edward Bagley is single... is one of eight children... founded the Bagley-Walden Foundation with the purpose of helping young people develop strategies for success through the utilization of athletic and academic programs... in the past, he has returned to Bridgeport during the summer to run a series of camps... at times, he's purchased a block of tickets for charitable use, known as the Bagley Bunch... most memorable Christmas: receiving his first pair of Pro Keds sneakers at the age of ten... majored in Sociology... shoe size is 12.

Career Highs: 35 points at Washington (2-4-85)
  11 rebounds at Boston (2-6-85)
  19 assists at Dallas (3-16-85)

TOP REGULAR SEASON PERFORMANCES

Points	Rebounds	Assists
14 vs. Phila at Htfd (11-14-89)	6 at Houston (2-13-90)	16 vs. Milwaukee (11-3-89)
13 vs. Milwaukee (11-3-89)	5 at Miami (4-7-90)	14 at Chicago (4-17-90)
12 vs. Minnesota (11-17-89)	5 vs. Detroit (3-30-90)	13 vs. Atlanta (11-10-89)
11 two times	4 two times	11 vs. New Jersey (4-4-90)

NBA CAREER RECORD

Year	Team	G	Min	FGM	FGA	Pct.	FTM	FTA	Pct	Off	Def	Tot	Ast	PF-Dq	St	Bl	Pts	Avg
82-83	Clev	68	990	161	373	.432	64	84	.762	17	79	96	167	74-0	54	5	386	5.7
83-84	Clev	76	1712	257	607	.423	157	198	.793	49	107	156	333	113-1	78	4	673	8.9
84-85	Clev	81	2401	338	693	.488	125	167	.749	54	237	291	697	132-0	129	5	804	9.9
85-86	Clev	78	2472	366	865	.423	170	215	.791	76	199	275	735	165-1	122	10	911	11.7
86-87	Clev	72	2182	312	732	.426	113	136	.831	55	197	252	379	114-0	91	7	768	10.7
87-88	N.J.	82	2774	393	896	.439	148	180	.822	61	196	257	479	162-0	110	10	981	12.0
88-89	N.J.	68	1642	200	481	.416	89	123	.724	36	108	144	391	117-0	72	5	500	7.4
89-90	Bos	54	1095	100	218	.459	29	39	.744	26	63	89	296	77-0	40	4	230	4.3
TOTALS		579	15268	2127	4865	.437	895	1142	.783	374	1186	1560	3477	954-2	696	50	5253	9.0

Three-Point Field Goals: 1982-83, 0-for-14; 1983-84, 2-for-17 (.118); 1984-85, 3-for-26 (.115); 1985-86, 9-for-37 (.243); 1986-87, 31-for-103 (.301); 1987-88, 47-for-161 (.292); 1988-89, 11-for-54 (.204); 1989-90, 1-for-18 (.056). Totals: 104-for-430 (.242).

PLAYOFF RECORD

Year	Team	G	Min	FGM	FGA	Pct.	FTM	FTA	Pct	Off	Def	Tot	Ast	PF-Dq	St	Bl	Pts	Avg
84-85	Clev	4	168	22	56	.393	7	10	.700	1	15	16	40	7-0	10	0	51	12.8
89-90	Bos	5	70	8	15	.533	3	4	.750	3	1	4	17	9-0	4	1	19	3.8
TOTALS		9	238	30	71	.423	10	14	.714	4	16	20	57	16-0	14	1	70	7.8

Three-Point Field Goals: 1984-85, 0-for-3; 1989-90, 0-for-1 (.000). Totals: 0-for-4 (.000).

SEASON/CAREER HIGHS

	FGM	FGA	FTM	FTA	REB	AST	ST	BL	PTS
1989-90/Regular Season	6/16	12/21	4/10	6/12	6/11	16/19	4/6	1/2	14/35
1990/Playoffs	5/11	7/19	2/4	2/6	1/7	5/15	1/5	1/1	10/22

LARRY BIRD

Birthdate: December 7, 1956
Birthplace: French Lick, IN
High School: Springs Valley (IN)
College: Indiana State '79
Height: 6-9
Weight: 220
Position: Forward
Years Pro: 11 Years

How Acquired: Celtics first-round draft choice in 1978... 6th pick overall.

1989-90 Season: Voted by NBA fans to the starting unit of the 1990 All-Star Game with 248,837 entries; only Michael Jordan received more votes... saw 23 mins in the ASG... participated in the Long Distance Shootout... in the season opener vs. the Bucks, he had 32 pts in 33 mins... in Chicago the next night, had the game winner with 3.6 secs left... 50 pts on 11/10 vs. Atlanta... had the game winner with 0.5 seconds left to defeat Philly in Hartford on 11/14... on 12/26, he made two fts with 0.2 seconds left to give Boston a one point win at the LAC... had 20 4th quarter points vs. Bulls on 3/4; had 20 4th qtr pts at Orlando, including the game winner with 27.1 seconds left (also had 0 to's) on 3/16... had 16 assts on 3/21... 10+ mins 75 times... 20+ mins 74 times... 30+ mins 69 times... 40+ mins 43 times... 10+ rebs 37 times... 10+ assts 17 times... 10+ pts 74 times, including his last 47 r/s games... 20+ pts 52 times... 30+ pts 16 times... 40+ pts 7 times... 50+ pts once... 34 double-doubles... 10 triple-doubles... started the first 30 games, and 45 straight from 1/13- 4/17... had the second best (Calvin Murphy, 78) free throw streak in NBA annals snapped at 71 on 2/13 in Houston; another was halted at 40 on 12/19... made 71 straight fts in the Garden from 11/24 thru 2/28 (missed vs. Mavs)... suffered a left ankle sprain vs. the LAC on 1/5; missed the next four games... did not attend the last three r/s games due to an abscess... overtook Bill Sharman as the best free throw shooter in Celtics' history... led the NBA in ft%... the only non-guard among the top 30 assists leaders, and his assists total was the second best of his career... in 15 games from 2/21 thru 3/23: 427 pts (172-313, 15-46, 70-75), 165 rebs, 113 assts, 28.5 ppg, .550 fg%; also had 20+ pts in each game... in his last 12 r/s BG games: 533 mins, 378 pts (143-269, 20-50, 72-75), and 31.5 ppg... 169 points in his last 5 BG games... during the playoffs, he was Boston's leading scorer (24.4), and registered a triple-double in Game One... tied for 10th in reg/sea MVP voting, finished in 9th place in the Allstate Goods Hands Award, and was a member of the All-NBA Second Team.

Professional Career: Drafted by Boston on the first-round of the 1978 draft, as a junior eligible, the 6th pick overall... voted the NBA Rookie of the Year in 1980 and was a member of the league's All-Rookie Team... a member of the All-NBA First Team his first nine years, and to the Second Team in his 11th... named to the All-Star Team his first nine years, ten total... named the All-Star Game MVP in 1982... All-Defensive Second Team in 1982, 1983, and 1984... playoff MVP in 1984 and 1986... regular season MVP in 1984, 1985, and 1986; one of only three players in NBA history to achieve the feat in three consecutive seasons ... Player of the Week 15 times... Player of the Month 7 times... NBA ft% leader in 1984, 1986, 1987, and 1990... Boston has never had a r/s losing month with him in the line-up... only Celtic to score 2,000+ points in three consecutive seasons... was held scoreless on 1/3/81 at Golden State... holds NBA playoff record for most points in one year, 1984... scored 10,000th career point on 1/11/85 vs. Washington... consecutive game-winning buzzer beaters on 1/27/85 (Portland) and 1/29/85 (Detroit)... set team mark with 60 pts on 3/12/85... 64 triple-doubles, including 55 in the r/s... 40+ points 49 times, 44 in the r/s... 50+ points 4 times, all in r/s... named AP Male Athlete of the Year for 1986... named The Sporting News Man of the Year for 1986... won the Long Distance Shootout in the first three years of its existence... triple-double in 1986 title clincher vs. Houston... consecutive 40+ games on 3/20/87 (Seattle) and 3/22/87 (New Jersey)... achieved a triple-double at halftime on 4/1/87 vs. Washington... made miraculous steal of Isiah Thomas' inbounds pass with five seconds left to give Boston a win in Game Five of their 1987 playoff series... on 11/7/87 at Wash, game-tying 3-pt fg with 4 secs left in reg; hit game-winner with 0 secs left in OT... on 11/11/87, he registered Boston's first 40/20 game (42 points and 20 rebs) vs. Indiana... first player in NBA history to register 50% fgs and 90% fts in the same season, and he is the only player to do it twice... when he plays 3,000 minutes in the r/s, Boston advances to the NBA Finals; when he doesn't play 3,000 minutes, Boston doesn't advance to the Finals... NBA's all-time 3-pt fg leader... missed all but six games in the 1988-89 season due to surgical removal of bone spurs in both heels... is the 15th best scorer in NBA history.

College Career: Consensus All-America in 1978 and 1979 and The Sporting News Player of the Year in 1979... TSN All-America First Team in 1978 and 1979... graduated as the fifth all-time leading NCAA scorer (30.3 ppg)... ISU compiled a record of 81-13 overall and 50-1 at home in his three years... led ISU to the 1979 NCAA Finals... John Wooden Award winner in 1979... also attended Indiana University, and Northwood Institute, but did not play.

Personal: Larry Joe Bird is married to the former Dinah Mattingly... has four brothers and one sister, mother's name is Georgia... brother Eddie plays basketball at ISU... avid outdoorsman... likes Kenny Rogers' music... fan of the St. Louis Cardinals... most memorable Christmas: all, because of family... returns to Indiana during the summer... owns "Larry Bird's Boston Connection," a hotel/restaurant in Terre Haute... on 8/2/84, a street in Terre Haute was named in his honor... holds the annual "Larry Bird Pro All-Star Scholarship Classic" during the off-season in Indiana... shoe size is 13 and a half.

TOP REGULAR SEASON PERFORMANCES

Points
60 vs. Atl. at N.O. (3-12-85)
53 vs. Indiana (3-30-83)
50 at Dallas (3-10-86)
50 vs. Atlanta (11-10-89)
49 vs. Washington (1-27-88)
49 at Phoenix (2-15-88)
48 three times

Rebounds
21 at Washington (3-16-82)
21 at Denver (12-29-81)
21 at LA Lakers (2-11-81)
21 at Philadelphia (11-1-80)
20 six times

Assists
17 at Golden State (2-16-84)
16 vs. Cleveland (3-21-90)
15 vs. Washington (4-1-87)
15 vs. Cleveland (3-27-85)
15 vs. Atlanta (1-13-82)
14 three times
13 eleven times

NBA RECORD

Year	Team	G	Min	FGM	FGA	Pct	FTM	FTA	Pct	Off	Def	Tot	Ast	PF-Dq	St	Bl	Pts	Avg
79-80	Bos.	82	2955	693	1463	.474	301	360	.836	216	636	852	370	279-4	143	53	1745	21.3
80-81	Bos.	82	3239	719	1503	.478	283	328	.863	191	704	895	451	239-2	161	63	1741	21.2
81-82	Bos.	77	2923	711	1414	.503	328	380	.863	200	637	837	447	244-0	143	66	1761	22.9
82-83	Bos.	79	2982	747	1481	.504	351	418	.840	193	677	870	458	197-0	148	71	1867	23.6
83-84	Bos.	79	3028	758	1542	.492	374	421	.888	181	615	796	520	197-0	144	69	1908	24.2
84-85	Bos.	80	3161	918	1760	.522	403	457	.882	164	678	842	531	208-0	129	98	2295	28.7
85-86	Bos.	82	3113	796	1606	.496	441	492	.896	190	615	805	557	182-0	166	51	2115	25.8
86-87	Bos.	74	3005	786	1497	.525	414	455	.910	124	558	682	566	185-3	135	70	2076	28.1
87-88	Bos.	76	2965	881	1672	.527	415	453	.916	108	595	703	467	157-0	125	57	2275	29.9
88-89	Bos.	6	189	49	104	.471	18	19	.947	1	36	37	29	18-0	6	5	116	19.3
89-90	Bos.	75	2944	718	1517	.473	319	343	.930	90	622	712	562	173-2	106	61	1820	24.3
TOTALS:		792	30504	7776	15559	.499	3647	4126	.883	1658	6373	803	4958	2079-11	1406	664	19719	24.9

Three-Point Field Goals: 1979-80, 58-for-143 (.406); 1980-81, 20-for-74 (.270); 1981-82, 11-for-52 (.212); 1982-83, 22-for-77 (.286); 1983-84, 18-for-73 (.247); 1984-85, 56-for-131 (.427); 1985-86, 82-for-194 (.423); 1986-87, 90-for-225 (.400); 1987-88, 98-for-237 (.414); 1988-89, 0-for-0 (.000); 1989-90, 65-for-195 (.333). Totals: 520-for-1401 (.371).

PLAYOFF RECORD

Year	Team	G	Min	FGM	FGA	Pct	FTM	FTA	Pct	Off	Def	Tot	Ast	PF-Dq	St	Bl	Pts	Avg
79-80	Bos.	9	372	83	177	.469	22	25	.880	22	79	101	42	30-0	14	8	192	21.3
80-81	Bos.	17	750	147	313	.470	76	85	.894	49	189	238	103	53-0	39	17	373	21.9
81-82	Bos.	12	490	88	206	.427	37	45	.822	33	117	150	67	43-0	23	17	214	17.8
82-83	Bos.	6	240	49	116	.422	24	29	.828	20	55	75	41	15-0	13	3	123	20.5
83-84	Bos.	23	961	229	437	.524	167	190	.879	62	190	252	136	71-0	54	27	632	27.5
84-85	Bos.	20	815	196	425	.461	121	136	.890	53	129	182	115	54-0	34	19	520	26.0
85-86	Bos.	18	770	171	331	.517	101	109	.927	34	134	168	148	55-0	37	11	466	25.9
86-87	Bos.	23	1015	216	454	.476	176	193	.912	41	190	231	165	55-1	27	19	622	27.0
87-88	Bos.	17	763	152	338	.450	101	113	.894	29	121	150	115	45-0	36	14	417	24.5
88-89	Bos.	0	0	0	0	.000	0	0	.000	0	0	0	0	0-0	0	0	0	0.0
89-90	Bos.	5	207	44	99	.444	29	32	.906	7	39	46	44	10-0	5	5	122	24.4
TOTALS:		150	6383	1375	2896	.475	854	957	.892	350	1243	1593	976	431-1	282	140	3681	24.5

Three-Point Field Goals: 1979-80, 4-for-15 (.267); 1980-81, 3-for-8 (.375); 1981-82, 1-for-6 (.167); 1982-83, 1-for-4 (.250); 1983-84, 7-for-17 (.412); 1984-85, 7-for-25 (.280); 1985-86, 23-for-56 (.411), 1986-87, 14-for-41 (.341); 1987-88, 12-for-32 (.375); 1988-89, 0-for-0 (.000); 1989-90, 5-for-19 (.263). Totals: 77-for-223 (.345).

ALL STAR GAME RECORD

Year	Team	Min	FGM	FGA	Pct	FTM	FTA	Pct	Off	Def	Tot	Ast	PF-Dq	St	Bl	Pts	Avg
1980	Bos.	23	3	6	.500	0	0	.000	3	3	6	7	1-0	1	0	7	7.0
1981	Bos.	18	1	5	.200	0	0	.000	1	3	4	10	1-0	1	0	2	2.0
1982	Bos.	28	7	12	.583	5	8	.625	0	12	12	5	3-0	1	1	19	19.0
1983	Bos.	29	7	14	.500	0	0	.000	3	10	13	7	4-0	2	0	14	14.0
1984	Bos.	33	6	18	.333	4	4	1.000	1	6	7	3	1-0	2	0	16	16.0
1985	Bos.	31	8	16	.500	5	6	.833	5	3	8	2	3-0	0	1	21	21.0
1986	Bos.	35	8	18	.444	5	6	.833	2	6	8	5	5-0	7	0	23	23.0
1987	Bos.	35	7	18	.389	4	4	1.000	2	4	6	5	5-0	2	0	18	18.0
1988	Bos.	32	2	8	.250	2	2	1.000	0	7	7	1	4-0	4	1	6	6.0
1990	Bos.	23	3	8	.375	2	2	1.000	2	6	8	3	1-0	3	0	8	8.0
TOTALS:		287	52	123	.423	27	32	.844	19	60	79	41	28-0	23	3	134	13.4

Three-Point Field Goals: 1980, 1-for-2 (.500); 1983, 0-for-1 (.000); 1985, 0-for-1 (.000); 1986, 2-for-4 (.500); 1987, 0-for-3 (.000); 1988, 0-for-1 (.000); 1990, 0-for-1 (.000). Totals: 3-for-13 (.231).

SEASON/CAREER HIGHS

	FGM	FGA	FTM	FTA	REB	AST	ST	BL	PTS
1989-90/Regular Season	19/22	33/36	13/15	13/17	18/21	16/17	5/9	5/5	50/60
1990/Playoffs	12/17	25/33	8/14	9/15	18/21	16/16	1/6	2/4	31/43

KEVIN GAMBLE

Birthdate: November 13, 1965
Birthplace: Springfield, IL
High School: Lanphier High (IL)
College: Iowa '87
Height: 6-5
Weight: 210
Position: Guard
Years Pro: 3 years

How Acquired: Signed as a free agent on December 15, 1989.

1989-90 Season: Started nine straight games from 11/7 thru 11/21; reserve role in the next 25... played in 15 straight from 1/21-2/21... played in eight straight from 3/14-3/28, including his 10th start on 3/27... 10+ mins in 22 of 24 from 12/19 thru 2/7... 10+ mins 46 times... 20+ mins 21 times... 30+ mins 2 times... 10+ pts 11 times... DNP-CD 11 times... scored 45 points in a three game stretch from 11/11-11/15... limited action during the playoffs.

Professional Career: Drafted by Portland on the third-round of the 1987 draft, the 63rd choice overall... began the 1987-88 season with the Blazers, playing nine games before being waived on December 9, 1987... joined the Quad City Thunder, and played in 40 games; he averaged 21.0 points, 5.9 rebounds, and 3.7 assists per game... finished third in the CBA Rookie of the Year voting... also played in the Phillipines with Anejo Rum... in 1988-89, he continued his play with Quad City and was the CBA's leading scorer (27.8 ppg in 12 contests) before his promotion to the Celtics... had a great stretch in the last six games of 1988-89 in which he averaged 22.8 ppg; in 6 starts, he had 137 points (57-87, 0-4, 23-30) in 235 minutes while adding 29 assists and 28 rebounds.

College Career: Played two years at Lincoln College in Lincoln, Illinois, and averaged 20.9 ppg... transferred to the University of Iowa, averaged 11.9 points and shot 54.4 percent from the field as a senior... played at Iowa under George Raveling and Tom Davis.

Personal: Kevin Douglas Gamble is single... received an Associate's Degree in Law Enforcement... lists shopping and playing video games as his hobbies... favorite foods are spaghetti and chili... enjoys the television show "Alf"... likes rap music... most influential person in his basketball life was Al Pickering, coach at Lincoln JC... names his mom as the most influential person in his private life... returns to Iowa in the summer... shoe size is 14.

TOP REGULAR SEASON PERFORMANCES

Points
31 vs. Charlotte (4-23-89)
27 at Indiana (4-21-89)
25 at Charlotte (4-17-89)
20 vs. Cleveland (4-14-89)

Rebounds
7 vs. Cleveland (4-14-89)
6 at Charlotte (4-17-89)
5 four times

Assists
10 vs. Cleveland (4-14-89)
7 at Charlotte (4-17-89)
6 vs. Charlotte (4-23-89)
6 vs LA Clippers (1-5-90)

NBA RECORD

Year	Team	G	Min	FGM	FGA	Pct	FTM	FTA	Pct	Off	Def	Tot	Ast	PF-Dq	St	Bl	Pts	Avg
87-88	Por.	9	19	0	3	.000	0	0	.000	2	1	3	1	2-0	2	0	0	0.0
88-89	Bos.	44	375	75	136	.551	35	55	.636	11	31	42	34	40-0	14	3	187	4.3
89-90	Bos.	71	990	137	301	.455	85	107	.704	42	70	112	119	77-1	28	8	362	5.1
TOTALS		124	1384	212	440	.481	120	162	.740	55	102	157	154	119-1	44	11	549	4.4

Three-Point Field Goals: 1987-88, 0-for-1 (.000); 1988-89, 2-for-11 (.182); 1989-90, 3-for-18 (.167). Totals: 5-for-30 (.167).

PLAYOFF RECORD

88-89	Bos.	1	29	4	11	.364	0	2	.000	1	0	1	2	1-0	1	0	8	8.0
89-90	Bos.	3	8	3	5	.600	0	0	.000	1	0	1	2	1-0	0	0	6	2.0
TOTALS		4	37	7	16	.438	0	2	.000	2	0	2	4	2-0	1	0	14	3.5

Three-Point Field Goals: 1988-89, 0-for-1 (.000); 1989-90, 0-for-0 (.000).
Totals: 0-for-1 (.000).

SEASON/CAREER HIGHS

	FGM	FGA	FTM	FTA	REB	AST	ST	BL	PTS
1989-90/Regular Season	6/13	12/18	6/9	6/12	5/7	6/10	4/4	1/2	18/31
1990/Playoffs	2/4	4/11	0/0	0/2	1/1	2/2	0/1	0/0	4/88

DENNIS JOHNSON

Birthdate: September 18, 1954
Birthplace: San Pedro, CA
High School: Dominguez High (CA)
College: Pepperdine '76
Height: 6-4
Weight: 202
Position: Guard
Years Pro: 14 Years

How Acquired: Traded by Phoenix with 1983 first and third-round draft choices to Boston for Rick Robey and two 1983 second- round draft choices on June 27, 1983.

1989-90 Season: Started 65 times during the regular season: all 3 games games from 11/8-11/11, 31 straight from 11/22-1/25, and 31 straight from 2/16-4/17... 10+ mins 71 times... 20+ mins 62 times... 30+ mins 34 times... 40+ mins 2 times... 10+ assts 12 times... 10+ pts 27 times... 20+ pts once ... 6 double-doubles... in two games against the Lakers: 73 mins, 34 pts (16-25, 2-2), 18 assts... 30+ mins/zero turnovers 4 times... suffered a grade two tear of the quadricep muscle in his right leg vs. NY, 1/31; prevented from playing in next four, returned to play on 2/13... missed the last three games due to a strained right calf suffered on 4/17 at Chicago... his fg% rose 23 points from 3/29 to the end of the regular season... made his last 27 ft's of the reg/ sea, and his last 34 including the playoffs... started all five playoff games... received a vote to the All- Defensive Team.

Professional Career: Drafted by Seattle on the second-round of the 1976 draft as a hardship case, the 29th pick overall... finished third in MVP balloting for the 1978-79 season... chosen the MVP of the 1979 playoffs, leading the Sonics to their only NBA championship... blocked 7 shots (2nd highest in the NBA Finals) at Washington on May 28, 1978... traded by Seattle to Phoenix for Paul Westphal on June 4, 1980... All-NBA Second Team in 1980... All-NBA First Team in 1981... selected to the All-Defensive First or Second Team for nine straight seasons; First Team member from 1979-1983 and 1987, and was a Second Team member from 1984-1986; only

Kareem Abdul-Jabbar has been named to the NBA All-Defensive Team more times... missed just one playoff game with Boston in seven years (Game Six of the 1984 Celtics-Knicks series)... scored his 10,000th career point on 11/23/84 vs. Washington... shares NBA record for most free throws made in one half of a championship series game (12), vs. Lakers on 6/12/84... hit a key buzzer-beating basket in Game Four of the 1985 Finals (6/5/85) tying that series at two games apiece... hit seven consecutive shots in Game One of the 1986 Celtics-Bulls series... hit a 75-foot basket in Game Two of the Celtics-Bucks 1986 playoff series (intended pass to Bird)... has been part of seven division championships, and three world championships (1979, 1984, 1986)... his teams have a combined regular season record of 753-395 (.656)... connected on a rare four-point play at Milwaukee on May 8, 1987... his basket with one second left (recipient of Larry Bird's tremendous steal) in Game Five of the 1987 playoff series vs. Detroit gave Boston an amazing win... scored 33 points in Game Six of the 1987 NBA Finals ... had a terrific postseason in 1988, including a triple-double in the opening round clincher in New York... became the 11th player in NBA history to register 15,000 points and 5,000 assists in a career; both were accomplished during the 1988-89 season.

College Career: Attended Los Angeles Harbor Junior College in Wilmington, California for two years... averaged 18.3 ppg in his second season... after Harbor JC, he spent one year at Pepperdine and on occasion played the center position... averaged 15.7 points per game in 1975-76, his sole season at Pepperdine.

Personal: Dennis Wayne Johnson and his wife Donna have a son, Dwayne (6/6/ 80)... nicknamed "DJ"... has 12 brothers and 3 sisters... returns to California during the summer... did not play high school basketball... admires actor Bill Cosby... he is co-chairman of the Boston "Sixty-Five Roses Club" benefitting the Cystic Fibrosis Foundation... involved with the Special Olympics and Governor's Alliance against drug use... his brother Joey attends Arizona State... shoe size is 12.

Career Highs: 39 points vs. New York (2-15-81)
12 rebounds vs. New Orleans (2-2-77)

TOP REGULAR SEASON PERFORMANCES

Points
30 vs. Indiana (11-13-85)
29 vs. Milwaukee (3-26-86)
29 at Portland (2-14-86)
29 at Indiana (1-2-86)
29 at Detroit (10-26-84)
10 vs. Detroit (11-27-83)

Rebounds
11 vs. Det. at Htfd. (1-29-85)
10 at Philadelphia (11-25-86)
10 at Atlanta (12-15-84)
10 vs. Detroit (11-2-84)
10 at Detroit (10-26-84)
13 five times

Assists
17 vs. Atl. at N.O. (3-12-85)
17 at Washington (11-7-87)
16 vs. LA Clippers (3-6-87)
15 vs. Denver (12-9-87)
14 two times

NBA RECORD

Year	Team	G	Min	FGM	FGA	Pct	FTM	FTA	Pct	Off	Def	Tot	Ast	PF-Dq	St	Bl	Pts	Avg
76-77	Sea.	81	1667	285	566	.504	179	287	.624	161	141	302	123	221-3	123	57	749	9.2
77-78	Sea.	81	2209	367	881	.417	297	406	.732	152	142	294	230	213-2	118	51	1031	12.7
78-79	Sea.	80	2717	482	1110	.434	306	392	.781	146	228	374	280	209-2	100	97	1270	15.9
79-80	Sea.	81	2937	574	1361	.422	380	487	.780	173	241	414	332	267-6	144	82	1540	19.0
80-81	Pho.	79	2615	532	1220	.436	411	501	.820	160	203	363	291	244-2	136	61	1486	18.8
81-82	Pho.	80	2937	577	1228	.470	399	495	.806	142	268	410	369	253-6	105	55	1561	19.5
82-83	Pho.	77	2551	398	861	.462	292	369	.791	92	243	335	388	204-1	97	39	1093	14.2
83-84	Bos.	80	2665	384	878	.437	281	330	.852	87	193	280	338	251-6	93	57	1053	13.2
84-85	Bos.	80	2976	493	1066	.462	261	306	.853	91	226	317	543	224-2	96	39	1254	15.7
85-86	Bos.	78	2732	482	1060	.455	243	297	.818	69	199	268	456	206-3	110	35	1213	15.6
86-87	Bos.	79	2933	423	953	.444	209	251	.833	45	216	261	594	201-0	87	38	1062	13.4
87-88	Bos.	77	2670	352	803	.438	255	298	.856	62	178	240	598	204-0	93	29	971	12.6
88-89	Bos.	72	2309	277	638	.434	160	195	.821	31	159	190	472	211-3	94	21	721	10.0
89-90	Bos.	75	2036	206	475	.434	118	140	.843	48	153	201	485	179-2	81	14	531	7.1
TOTALS:		1100	35954	5832	13100	.445	3791	4754	.797	1459	2790	4249	5499	3087-38	1477	675	15535	14.1

Three-Point Field Goals: 1979-80, 12-for-58 (.207); 1980-81, 11-for-51 (.216); 1981-82, 8-for-42 (.190); 1982-83, 5-for-31 (.161); 1983-84, 4-for-32 (.125); 1984-85, 7-for-26 (.269); 1985-86, 6-for-42 (.143); 1986-87, 7-for-62 (.113); 1987-88, 12-for-46 (.261); 1988-89, 7-for-50 (.140); 1989-90, 1-for-24 (.042).
Totals: 73-for-414 (.176).

PLAYOFF RECORD

Year	Team	G	Min	FGM	FGA	Pct	FTM	FTA	Pct	Off	Def	Tot	Ast	PF-Dq	St	Bl	Pts	Avg
77-78	Sea.	22	827	121	294	.412	112	159	.704	47	54	101	72	63-0	23	23	354	16.1
78-79	Sea.	17	691	136	302	.450	84	109	.771	44	60	104	69	63-0	28	26	356	20.9
79-80	Sea.	15	582	100	244	.410	52	62	.839	25	39	64	57	48-2	27	10	257	17.1
80-81	Pho.	7	267	52	110	.473	32	42	.762	7	26	33	20	18-0	9	9	137	19.6
81-82	Pho.	7	271	63	132	.477	30	39	.769	13	18	31	32	28-2	15	4	156	22.3
82-83	Pho.	3	108	22	48	.458	10	12	.833	6	17	23	17	9-0	5	2	54	18.0
83-84	Bos.	22	808	129	319	.404	104	120	.867	30	49	79	97	75-1	25	7	365	16.6
84-85	Bos.	21	848	142	319	.445	80	93	.860	24	60	84	154	66-0	31	9	364	17.3
85-86	Bos.	18	715	109	245	.445	67	84	.798	23	53	76	107	58-2	39	5	291	16.2
86-87	Bos.	23	964	168	361	.465	96	113	.850	24	67	91	205	71-0	16	8	435	18.9
87-88	Bos.	17	702	91	210	.433	82	103	.796	15	62	77	139	51-0	24	8	270	15.9
88-89	Bos.	3	59	4	15	.267	0	0	0	2	2	4	9	8-0	3	0	8	2.7
89-90	Bos.	5	162	30	62	.484	7	7	1.000	2	12	14	28	17-1	2	2	69	13.8
TOTALS:		180	7004	1167	2661	.439	756	943	.802	262	519	781	1006	575-8	247	113	3116	17.3

Three-Point Field Goals: 1979-80, 5-for-15 (.333); 1980-81, 1-for-5 (.200); 1981-82, 0-for-3 (.000); 1982-83, 0-for-1 (.000); 1983-84, 3-for-7 (.429); 1984-85, 0-for-14 (.000); 1985-86, 6-for-16 (.357); 1986-87, 3-for-26 (.115);1987-88, 6-for-16 (.375). 1988-89, 0-for-0 (.000); 1989-90, 2-for-6 (.333). Totals: 26-for-109 (.239).

ALL STAR GAME RECORD

Year	Team	Min	FGM	FGA	Pct	FTM	FTA	Pct	Off	Def	Tot	Ast	PF-Dq	St	Bl	Pts	Avg
1979	Sea.	27	5	7	.714	2	2	1.000	1	0	1	3	30	0	1	12	12.0
1980	Sea.	20	7	13	.538	5	6	.833	2	2	4	1	30	2	1	19	19.0
1981	Pho.	24	5	8	.625	9	10	.900	1	1	2	1	10	3	0	19	19.0
1982	Pho.	15	0	2	.000	1	2	.500	2	3	5	1	10	0	2	1	1.0
1985	Bos.	12	3	7	.429	2	2	1.000	1	5	6	3	20	0	0	8	8.0
TOTALS:		98	20	37	.541	19	22	.864	7	11	18	9	100	5	4	59	11.8

SEASON/CAREER HIGHS

	FGM	FGA	FTM	FTA	REB	AST	ST	BL	PTS
1989-90/Regular Season	11/14	15/29	8/16	11/18	9/12	14/17	4/6	2/5	24/39
1990/Playoffs	10/13	20/27	4/13	4/17	5/12	10/17	1/7	2/7	21/33

JOE KLEINE

Birthdate: January 4, 1962
Birthplace: Colorado Springs, CO
High School: Slater High (Slater, MO)
College: Arkansas '85
Height: 7-0
Weight: 271
Position: Center
Years Pro: 5 years

How Acquired: Traded by Sacramento with Ed Pinckney to Boston for Danny Ainge and Brad Lohaus on February 23, 1989.

1989-90 Season: In his first full season as a Celtic, he was chosen the SportsChannel/Texaco Sixth Man of the Year, emblematic of the individual who best displays Celtics' Pride... participated in every game but one (DNP-CD on 3/4 vs. Bulls)... reserve in the first 56 games... 10+ mins 72 times... 20+ mins 25 times... 30+ mins 5 times... 10+ rebs 6 times... 10+ pts 14 times... 5 double-doubles... 14 pts/12 rebs at Bulls 11/4... 27 pts/21 rebs in consecutive reserve roles on 12/29 and 1/3... hit the game winning fg with 8.2 secs left vs. Philly, 3/11... his fg% was a career high ... in his first 89-90 start, he had 18 pts and held Moses Malone to 4 pts (1-7 fgs), 3/13... 4 straight starts from 3/13-3/18: 116 mins, 45 pts (17- 33, 11-11), and 23 rebs... made 25 straight fts from 3/11-4/1... played in all five playoff games, and made 76.5% of his fgs.

Professional Career: Drafted by Sacramento on the first-round of the 1985 draft, the sixth player taken overall... started 18 of his 80 appearances in his rookie season... played in all 82 games in 1987-88, including starts in 60... was the Kings second best rebounder in 1987-88... his minutes, field goals made, attempted, and percentage, free throws made, attempted, and percentage, offensive, defensive, and total rebounds, assists, blocks, points, and scoring average all increased in his first three years... missed just nine games in three-plus seasons with the Kings... in 1988-89, he started 11 times in 47 appearances for Sacramento... was a 92% free throw shooter in 1988-89 with Sacramento.

College Career: Played his freshman season with Notre Dame and made 64% of his fgs (32-50)... transferred to Arkansas... sat out the entire 1981-82 season... chosen Southwest Conference Newcomer of the Year in his first season with the Razorbacks, averaging 13.3 ppg and 7.3 rpg in 1982-83... Arkansas' top scorer in his junior and senior years... ppg increased all four years... member of the 1984 US Olympic Team... member of the 1982 World University Games Team... graduated as the fourth best scorer in Arkansas' history (1,753).

Personal: Joseph William Kleine and his wife Dana have one child, Daniel Christopher (2/23/89), born the day of his father's trade to Boston... college teammate of Alvin Robertson, Darrell Walker, Scott Hastings, and Tony Brown... likes to fish, golf, and read... involved with the Leukemia Society, Big Brothers and Big Sisters, and People Reaching Out organizations... favorite television shows: "M*A*S*H" and "The Andy Griffith Show"... lists Dallas (besides Boston) as his favorite NBA city... spends his summer in both Dallas and Arkansas... names his dad as his most influential person... graduated with a degree in Business Administration... most memorable Christmas: Christmas '89, because it was his son's first... shoe size is 16.

Career Highs: 23 points at LA Clippers (3-20-88) 23 points vs. LA Clippers (4-2-88) 18 rebounds vs. Chicago (12-3-85) 8 assists vs. LA Clippers (4-2-87)

TOP REGULAR SEASON PERFORMANCES

Points	Rebounds	Assists
18 at Atlanta (3-13-90)	13 vs. Washington (1-3-90)	4 vs. Houston (3-31-89)
16 vs. Houston (3-31-89)	12 at Chicago (11-4-89)	4 vs. Portland (3-29-89)
16 vs. Charlotte (2-7-90)	11 vs. Orlando (4-18-90)	3 at Atlanta (4-13-89)
15 at Seattle (12-29-89)	11 vs. Houston (3-31-89)	3 vs. Orlando (4-18-90)

NBA RECORD

Year	Team	G	Min	FGM	FGA	Pct	FTM	FTA	Pct	Off	Def	Tot	Ast	PF-Dq	St	Bl	Pts	Avg
85-86	Sac.	80	1180	160	344	.465	94	130	.723	113	260	373	46	224-1	24	34	414	5.2
86-87	Sac.	79	1658	256	543	.471	110	140	.786	173	310	483	71	213-2	35	30	622	7.9
87-88	Sac.	82	1999	324	686	.472	153	188	.814	179	400	579	93	228-1	28	59	801	9.8
88-89	Sac/Bos	75	1411	175	432	.405	134	152	.882	124	254	378	67	192-2	33	23	484	6.5
89-90	Bos.	81	1365	176	367	.480	83	100	.830	117	238	355	46	170-0	15	27	435	5.4
TOTALS:		397	7613	1091	2372	.459	574	710	.808	706	1462	2168	323	1027-6	135	173	2756	6.9

Three-Point Field Goals:1986-87, 0-for-1 (.000); 1988-89, 0-for-2 (.000);1989-90, 0-for-4 (.000). Totals: 0-for-7 (.000).

PLAYOFF RECORD

Year	Team	G	Min	FGM	FGA	Pct	FTM	FTA	Pct	Off	Def	Tot	Ast	PF-Dq	St	Bl	Pts	Avg
85-86	Sac.	3	45	5	13	.385	5	6	.833	8	6	14	1	8-0	1	1	15	5.0
88-89	Bos.	3	65	6	11	.545	7	9	.778	4	13	17	2	9-0	0	1	19	6.3
89-90	Bos.	5	79	13	17	.765	5	6	.833	3	11	14	2	12-0	2	3	31	6.2
TOTALS:		11	189	24	41	.585	17	21	.810	15	30	45	5	29-0	3	5	65	5.9

Three-Point Field Goals:1988-89, 0-for-1 (.000); 1989-90, 0-for-1 (.000). Totals: 0-for-2 (.000).

SEASON/CAREER HIGHS

	FGM	FGA	FTM	FTA	REB	AST	ST	BL	PTS
1989-90/Regular Season	7/10	14/17	4/8	6/9	13/18	3/8	2/3	2/3	18/23
1990/Playoffs	4/4	5/6	3/6	4/7	6/11	1/1	1/1	1/1	11/12

REGGIE LEWIS

Birthdate: November 21, 1965
Birthplace: Baltimore, MD
High School: Dunbar High (MD)
College: Northeastern '87
Height.: 6-7
Weight: 195
Position: Guard-Forward
Years Pro: 3 Years

How Acquired: Celtics first-round draft choice in 1987... 22nd pick overall.

1989-90 Season: Started 54 times in his third pro season: all 3 from 11/22-11/25, 37 straight from 1/6-3/24, and the final 14 regular season games... had a fine season opener with 26 pts (12-16, 2-2) in 28 mins vs. Milwaukee as a reserve... 10+ mins 78 times... 20+ mins 73 times... 30+ mins 51 times ... 40+ mins 12 times... 10+ pts 67 times... 20+ pts 29 times... 30+ pts 3 times... 10+ rebs 3 times... 3 double-doubles... suffered a strained left hamstring on 12/8; missed games on 12/9 and 12/13... did not dress at Indiana on 3/27 due to a sprained right ankle... 9-11 fgs vs. Nets, 24 pts, 11/15... 32 pts/11 rebs vs. Detroit, 1/10... 10-13 fgs at Lakers, 2/18... 11-13 fgs at Bulls, 4/17... Boston went 25-4 when he scored 20+ pts in the reg/sea... scored 235 pts in the last 10 regular season games... had career highs in field goal%, free throw%, and assists total... in five playoff starts, he made 59.7% of his fgs, and averaged 20.2 ppg.

Professional Career: Drafted by Boston on the first-round of the 1987 draft, the 22nd pick overall... saw limited duty in his first NBA season... best stretch in 1987-88 was a five game span from 11/15-11/21 as he scored 49 total points... in 1988-89, he started 57 times in the small forward position, replacing the injured Larry Bird... chosen the SportsChannel Sixth Man of the Year in 1988-89... finished second to Phoenix' Kevin Johnson in the NBA's Most Improved Player voting (1988-89)... his fg% and ft% have increased each season.

College Career: Four year starter at Northeastern... all-time Huskies leading scorer with 2,708 points (22.2); graduated as the ninth all-time NCAA Division One scorer... all-time leading shot blocker in Huskie history with 155... led Northeastern to four consecutive ECAC North Atlantic Conference titles as well as four straight trips to the NCAA Tournament... earned ECAC North Atlantic Conference Rookie of the Year honors... first ever three-time ECAC NAC Player of the Year, '85, '86, '87... the Huskies went 102-26 in his four years on Huntington Avenue, with a 72-6 conference record during that span... tri-captain in junior and senior years... had his jersey (number 35) retired in ceremonies on 1/21/89.

Personal: Reggie Lewis is single... played high school ball with NBA players Reggie Williams, Tyrone Bogues, and David Wingate... most memorable Christmas: when his mom made him open the gifts on Christmas Eve, something he had always wanted to do ... considers his mom as the most influential person in his life... maintains residence year-round in the Boston area... as a youngster, he admired George Gervin... shoe size is 13.

TOP REGULAR SEASON PERFORMANCES

Points
39 at Philadelphia (3-28-89)
35 vs. Portland (3-29-89)
34 vs. New York (4-15-90)
33 at Chicago (12-6-88)
32 three times

Rebounds
12 vs. Cleveland (4-14-89)
11 at Sacramento (2-22-89)
11 vs. Detroit (1-10-90)
10 three times

Assists
9 vs. Orlando (4-18-90)
9 at LA Lakers (2-18-90)
8 vs. LA Clippers (1-5-90)
6 nine games

NBA RECORD

Year	Team	G	Min	FGM	FGA	Pct	FTM	FTA	Pct	Off	Def	Tot	Ast	PF-Dq	St	Bl	Pts	Avg
87-88	Bos.	49	405	90	193	.466	40	57	.702	28	35	63	26	54-0	16	15	220	4.5
88-89	Bos.	81	2657	604	1242	.486	284	361	.787	116	261	377	218	258-5	124	72	1495	18.5
89-90	Bos.	79	2522	540	1089	.496	256	317	.808	109	238	347	225	216-2	88	63	1340	17.0
TOTALS:		209	5584	1234	2524	.488	580	735	.789	253	534	787	469	528-7	228	150	3055	14.6

Three-Point Field Goals:1987-88, 0-for-4 (.000); 1988-89, 3-for-22 (.136);1989-90, 4-for-15 (.267).
Totals: 7-for-41 (.171).

PLAYOFF RECORD

Year	Team	G	Min	FGM	FGA	Pct	FTM	FTA	Pct	Off	Def	Tot	Ast	PF-Dq	St	Bl	Pts	Avg
87-88	Bos.	12	70	13	34	.382	3	5	.600	9	7	16	4	13-0	3	2	29	2.4
88-89	Bos.	3	125	26	55	.473	9	13	.692	5	16	21	11	11-0	5	0	61	20.3
89-90	Bos.	5	200	37	62	.597	27	35	.771	9	16	25	22	14-0	7	2	101	20.2
TOTALS:		20	395	76	151	.503	39	53	.736	23	39	62	37	38-0	15	4	191	9.6

Three-Point Field Goals: 1987-88, 0-for-1 (.000); 1988-89, 0-for-2 (.000); 1989-90, 0-for-1 (.000).Totals: 0-for-4 (.000).

SEASON/CAREER HIGHS

	FGM	FGA	FTM	FTA	REB	AST	ST	BL	PTS
1989-90/Regular Season	13/16	27/30	11/11	15/15	11/12	9/9	4/5	4/4	34/39
1990/Playoffs	9/10	13/21	8/8	10/10	8/8	9/9	3/3	1/1	23/23

KEVIN McHALE

Birthdate: December 19, 1957
Birthplace: Hibbing (MN)
High School: Hibbing High (MN)
College: Minnesota '80
Height: 6-10
Weight: 225
Position: Forward-Center
Years Pro: 10 Years

How Acquired: Celtics first-round draft choice in 1980... 3rd pick overall.

1989-90 Season: Named to the Eastern Conference All-Star reserves; had 13 pts (6-11, 1-1, 0-0) and 8 rebs in 20 mins... only Celtic to play in all 82 games... appeared in the first 32 games as a reserve, before starting on 1/10 and 1/12; reserve in the next 25, before starting the final 23 regular season games... 10+ pts streak snapped at 247 straight reg/sea contests; had 9 pts at Detroit, 11/18... 10+ mins 82 times... 20+ mins 82 times... 30+ mins 58 times... 40+ mins 11 times... 10+ rebs 29 times... 29 double-doubles... 10+ pts 78 times... 20+ pts 49 times... 30+ pts 11 times... had a career best free throw streak snapped at 44 on 12/13; had another streak snapped at 31 on 2/18, and ended the regular season by converting his final 32 (last missed on March 6)... had his finest season from the charity stripe... ft% was at .930 after the 2/25 game... became the first player to finish in the top ten in fg% and ft% in the same season since Lou Hudson did so for Atlanta in 1969-70... 23-65 3-ptrs in the last 42 games; 0-for-4 in the first 40 games... 3-3 from 3-pt land at Golden State on 2/23... scored 279 pts in 10 games from 3/9-3/27... registered blocks (5+ 3 times in the last seven) in the last 22 regular season games... in five post-season starts, he averaged 22.0 ppg, and made 60.9% of his shots... received 33 votes to the All-NBA Team, and was also chosen by media members to the All-Interview First Team.

Professional Career: Drafted by Boston on the first-round of the 1980 draft after Golden State took Joe Barry Carroll and Utah chose Darrell Griffith... came extremely close to playing in Italy (with Trieste) before signing with the Celtics in September, 1980... named to the NBA All-Rookie Team in 1981... preserved Boston's win in Game Six of Celtics-Sixers 1981 playoff series by blocking Andrew Toney's shot and then grabbing the rebound in the final seconds... started 32 times in the 1981-82

season... named to the All-Defensive Second Team in 1983, 1989, and 1990... named to the All-Defensive First Team in 1986, 1987, and 1988... recipient of NBA's Sixth Man Award in 1984 and 1985... started 31 times in 1984-85, including 26 consecutive starts from 2/18-4/11... scored 56 points vs. Detroit on March 3, 1985 for what was then a team record... shares team record for field goals made in a game with 22... scored 42 points in New York in game following 56 point effort; 98 points in consecutive games is a team record... once played in 413 consecutive games before missing on 12/21/84... became starter in frontcourt when Celtics dealt Cedric Maxwell to the LA Clippers on 9/6/85... suffered a sore left Achilles in the 1985-86 season, causing him to miss 14 games... Boston's leading scorer in the 1985 and 1986 NBA Finals... 30+ points in 61 regular season games... became the first player in NBA history to shoot 60% from the floor and 80% from the free throw line in one season in 1986-87... became the fourth Celtic to register 2,000 points in a season when he accomplished that in 1986-87... finished among the NBA's top ten field goal shooters in each of the last six years, including first place finishes in 1986-87 and 1987-88... began the 1987-88 season on the injured list due to right foot surgery... scored the 10,000th point of his career on 1/12/88... hit a game-tying three-point field goal with 5 seconds left in the first overtime of Game Two of the Celtics-Pistons Eastern Conference Finals (5/26/88)... became the eighth Celtic to grab 5,000 rebounds, on 2/1/89.

College Career: First Team All-Big Ten selection by AP and UPI in 1979-80... graduated as Minnesota's second leading scorer (1,704 points) and rebounder (950)... team MVP in 1980... MVP of the Pillsbury Classic three times... MVP of the Aloha Classic in 1980... starter on the Gold Medal-winning Pan American Team in the summer of 1979... started on the Gold Medal-winning World University Games Team in 1979... named to the All-Big Ten Team for the decade of the 1970's.

Personal: Kevin Edward McHale and wife Lynn have four children, Kristyn (5/9/83), Michael (2/23/85), Joseph (12/10/86), and Alexandra (10/27/89)... likes to golf, fish, and play backgammon... loves hockey, and is a fan of the Boston Bruins... returns to Minnesota in the summer... enjoys the music of Bruce Springsteen and Bob Dylan... lists his father as his most influential person... as a youngster, his favorite athlete was Jack Nicklaus... shoe size is 15 and a half.

TOP REGULAR SEASON PERFORMANCES

Points
56 vs. Detroit (3-3-85)
42 at New York (3-5-85)
38 vs. Detroit (3-1-87)
38 vs. Cleveland (1-16-87)
37 two times

Rebounds
18 at L.A. Clippers (12-30-85)
18 at Detroit (1-16-89)
17 at Cleveland (1-23-88)
17 vs. Indiana (3-11-88)
17 vs. Golden State (11-21-86)

Assists
10 vs. Dallas (4-3-88)
9 vs. Philadelph ia (3-25-88)
8 at New Jersey (4-9-86)
7 five times
6 twelve times

NBA RECORD

Year	Team	G	Min	FGM	FGA	Pct	FTM	FTA	Pct	Off	Def	Tot	Ast	PF-Dq	St	Bl	Pts	Avg
80-81	Bos.	82	1645	355	666	.533	108	159	.679	155	204	359	55	260-3	27	151	818	10.0
81-82	Bos.	82	2332	465	875	.531	187	248	.754	191	365	556	91	264-1	30	185	1117	13.6
82-83	Bos.	82	2345	483	893	.541	193	269	.717	215	338	553	104	241-3	34	192	1159	14.1
83-84	Bos.	82	2577	587	1055	.556	336	439	.765	208	402	610	104	243-5	23	126	1511	18.4
84-85	Bos.	79	2653	605	1062	.570	355	467	.760	229	483	712	141	234-3	28	120	1565	19.8
85-86	Bos.	68	2397	561	978	.574	326	420	.776	171	380	551	181	192-2	29	134	1448	21.3
86-87	Bos.	77	3060	790	1307	.604	428	512	.836	247	516	763	198	240-1	38	172	2008	26.1
87-88	Bos.	64	2390	550	911	.604	346	434	.797	159	377	536	171	179-1	27	92	1446	22.6
88-89	Bos.	78	2876	661	1211	.546	436	533	.818	223	414	637	172	223-2	26	97	1758	22.5
89-90	Bos.	82	2722	648	1181	.549	393	440	.893	201	476	677	172	250-3	30	157	1712	20.9
TOTALS:		776	24997	5705	10139	.562	3108	3921	.792	1999	3955	5954	1289	2326-24	292	1426	14542	18.7

Three-PointField Goals: 1980-81,0-for-2(.000);1982-83,0-for-1 (.000);1983-84,1-for-3 (.333);1984-85,0-for-6(.000); 1986-87,0-for-4(.000);1988-89,0-for-4 (.000); 1989-90,23-for-69 (.333).
Totals: 24-for-89 (.270).

PLAYOFF RECORD

Year	Team	G	Min	FGM	FGA	Pct	FTM	FTA	Pct	Off	Def	Tot	Ast	PF-Dq	St	Bl	Pts	Avg
80-81	Bos.	17	296	61	113	.540	23	36	.639	29	30	59	14	51-1	4	25	145	8.5
81-82	Bos.	12	344	77	134	.575	40	53	.755	41	44	85	11	44-0	5	27	194	16.2
82-83	Bos.	7	177	34	62	.548	10	18	.556	15	27	42	5	16-0	3	7	78	11.1
83-84	Bos.	23	702	123	244	.504	94	121	.777	62	81	143	27	75-1	3	35	340	14.8
84-85	Bos.	21	837	172	303	.568	121	150	.807	74	134	208	32	73-3	13	46	465	22.1
85-86	Bos.	18	715	168	290	.579	112	141	.794	51	104	155	48	64-0	8	43	448	24.9
86-87	Bos.	21	827	174	298	.584	96	126	.762	66	128	194	39	71-2	7	30	444	21.1
87-88	Bos.	17	716	158	262	.603	115	137	.839	55	81	136	40	65-1	7	30	432	25.4
88-89	Bos.	3	115	20	41	.448	17	23	.739	7	17	24	9	13-0	1	2	57	19.0
89-90	Bos.	5	192	42	69	.609	25	29	.862	8	31	39	13	17-0	2	10	110	22.0
TOTALS:		144	4921	1029	1816	.567	653	834	.783	408	677	1085	238	489-8	53	255	2713	18.8

Three-Point Field Goals: 1982-83,0-for-1(.000);1983-84, 0-for-3(.000);1985-86,0-for-1 (.000);1987-88, 1-for-1(1.000); 1989-90,1-for-3 (.333).
Totals: 2-for-9 (.000).

ALL STAR RECORD

Year	Team	Min	FGM	FGA	Pct	FTM	FTA	Pct	Off	Def	Tot	Ast	PF-Dq	St	Bl	Pts	Avg
1984	Bos.	11	3	7	.429	4	6	.667	2	3	5	0	1-0	0	0	10	10.0
1986	Bos.	20	3	38	.375	2	2	1.000	3	7	10	2	4-0	0	4	8	8.0
1987	Bos.	30	7	11	.636	2	2	1.000	4	3	7	2	5-0	0	4	16	16.0
1988	Bos.	14	0	1	.000	2	2	1.000	0	1	1	1	2-0	0	2	2	2.0
1989	Bos.	16	5	7	.714	0	0	.000	1	2	3	0	3-0	0	2	10	10.0
1990	Bos.	20	6	11	.545	0	0	.000	2	6	8	1	4-0	0	0	13	13.0
TOTALS:		111	24	45	.533	10	12	.833	12	22	34	6	19-0	0	12	59	9.8

Three-Point Field Goals: 1990,1-for-1 (1.000).

SEASON /CAREER HIGHS

	FGM	FGA	FTM	FTA	REB	AST	ST	BL	PTS
1989-90/Regular Season	14/22	24/30	14/15	15/19	14/18	7/10	2/3	6/9	34/56
1990/Playoffs	12/15	15/25	8/14	9/16	10/17	5/7	2/3	3/6	31/34

ROBERT PARISH

Birthdate: August 30, 1953
Birthplace: Shreveport, LA
High School: Woodlawn (Shreveport, LA)
College: Centenary '76
Height: 7-1/2
Weight: 230
Position: Center
Years Pro: 14 Years

How Acquired: Traded by Golden State with a 1980 first-round draft choice for two 1980 first-round draft choices on June 9, 1980.

1989-90 Season: Named to the Eastern Conference All-Star reserves; had 14 pts (7-11, 0-1) and 4 rebs in 21 mins, and tied for second place in the MVP voting... 31 points (12-14, 7-10) with 17 rebs at the Cavs on 11/11...10-12 fgs at Hawks on 11/25... in two games vs. the Lakers: 79 mins, 43 pts (19-28, 5-9), 24 rebs... made all 7 fgs on 12/5 at Hornets... scored 38 pts (tied for second best of career) on 12/8 vs. Denver... 29 pts (12-15 fgs) at the Bullets on 1/6... had three key rebs in last minute vs. Knicks, on 1/31...10+ mins 78 times... 20+ mins 74 times... 30+ mins 44 times... 40+ mins 5 times...10+ rebs 44 times... 10+ pts 65 times... 20+ pts 17 times... 30+ pts 3 times... 43 double-doubles... surpassed the 18,000 point mark on 3/7... made 21 straight fts from 2/25-3/21... started 78 times, including the first 60 games and the regular season's final 18... suffered a hyperextended right knee vs. Philly on 3/11, causing him to miss the next three games... returned to action on 3/18... shot 49-70 (.700) from the field in the last six games of March... his fg% was the second highest of his career... started all five playoff games, averaging 15.8 ppg; made 17 of 18 fts, and led Boston with 50 rebounds... received a pair of votes to the All-NBA team.

Professional Career: Drafted by Golden State on the first-round of the 1976 draft, the 8th pick overall... had an incredible game on 3/30/79 against the Knicks when he scored 30 points and grabbed 32 rebounds... traded to Boston along with a pick that turned out to be Kevin McHale; in return, Boston traded two number one picks to the Warriors, which selected Joe Barry Carroll and Rickey Brown... became Boston's force in the middle when Dave Cowens suddenly retired... runner-up to Larry Bird in the 1982 All-Star MVP balloting... shares the team record with 9 blocks on 3/17/82... named to the All-NBA Second Team in 1982... scored the 10,000th point of his career on 2/26/84 in Phoenix... had two key steals in the waning moments of overtime in Game Two of the 1984 Finals... represented the Celtics in the All-Star Game eight times... played in 99 of 100 games in the 1985-86 season... is the only Celtic to grab 25+ rebounds in a game (accomplished twice) since the 1977-78 season... registered his lone triple-double on 3/29/87 vs. the Sixers... missed Game Six of the 1987 series at Milwaukee, snapping a streak of 116 straight playoff appearances... finished second to teammate Kevin McHale in field goal accuracy during the 1987-88 season; in fact, he has been in the NBA's top ten in each of the past six years... grabbed his 10,000th rebound on 2/22/89... named to the All-NBA Third Team in 1989.

College Career: Named to The Sporting News All-America First Team in 1976... a Gold Medalist in the 1975 World University Games, a team coached by Dave Gavitt... played four years at Centenary... once had 50 points in a game against So. Miss... grabbed 33 rebounds in a game... averaged 21.6 points in 108 career games... averaged 23.0 points as a freshman, and 24.8 as a senior... made 56.4% of his fgs.

Personal: Robert L. Parish is single... relaxes to jazz music... other enjoyments include judo, backgammon and horror films... nicknamed "Chief" by Cedric Maxwell, after a character in "One Flew Over the Cuckoo's Nest"... resides in the Boston area year-round... went to the same high school as former NFL star Terry Bradshaw... holds a basketball camp at New Hampshire College during the summer... most memorable Christmas moment: the spirit of giving and receiving with his family as a youngster... lists Bill Russell, Wilt Chamberlain, and Clifford Ray as his favorite athletes... names his dad as his most influential person... shoe size is 16.

Career Highs: 32 rebounds vs. New York (3-30-79).

TOP REGULAR SEASON PERFORMANCES

Points
40 at San Antonio (2-17-81)
38 vs. Houston (3-17-85)
38 vs. Denver (12-8-89)
37 at Philadelphia (3-21-82)

Rebounds
25 vs. Sacramento (1-9-87)
25 at Washington (3-8-86)
24 at Charlotte (2-1-89)
23 two times

Assists
10 vs. Philadelphia (3-29-87)
9 at Detroit (11-15-86)
7 at Chicago (1-21-83)
7 vs. Seattle (2-5-89)

NBA RECORD

Year	Team	G	Min	FGM	FGA	Pct	FTM	FTA	Pct	Off	Def	Tot	Ast	PF-Dq	St	Bl	Pts	Avg
76-77	G.S.	77	1384	288	573	.503	121	171	.708	201	342	543	74	224-7	55	94	697	9.1
77-78	G.S.	82	1969	430	911	.472	165	264	.625	211	469	680	95	291-10	79	123	1025	12.5
78-79	G.S.	76	2411	554	1110	.499	196	281	.698	265	651	916	115	303-10	100	217	1304	17.2
79-80	G.S.	72	2119	510	1006	.507	203	284	.715	247	536	783	122	248-6	58	115	1223	17.0
80-81	Bos.	82	2298	635	1166	.545	282	397	.710	245	532	777	144	310-9	81	214	1552	18.9
81-82	Bos.	80	2534	669	1235	.542	252	355	.710	288	578	866	140	267-5	68	192	1590	19.9
82-83	Bos.	78	2459	619	1125	.550	271	388	.698	260	567	827	141	222-4	79	148	1509	19.3
83-84	Bos.	80	2867	623	1140	.546	274	368	.745	243	614	857	139	266-7	55	116	1520	19.0
84-85	Bos.	79	2850	551	1016	.542	292	393	.743	263	577	840	125	223-2	56	101	1394	17.6
85-86	Bos.	81	2567	530	966	.549	245	335	.731	246	524	770	145	215-3	65	116	1305	16.1
86-87	Bos.	80	2995	588	1057	.556	227	309	.735	254	597	851	173	266-5	64	144	1403	17.5
87-88	Bos.	74	2312	442	750	.589	177	241	.734	173	455	628	115	198-5	55	84	1061	14.3
88-89	Bos.	80	2840	596	1045	.570	294	409	.719	342	654	996	175	209-2	79	116	1486	18.6
89-90	Bos.	79	2396	505	871	.580	233	312	.747	259	537	796	103	189-2	38	69	1243	15.7
TOTALS:		1100	34001	7540	13971	.539	3232	4507	.717	3497	7633	11130	1806	3431-77	932	1849	18312	16.6

Three-Point Field Goals: 1979-80, 0-for-1 (.000); 1980-81, 0-for-1 (.000); 1982-83, 0-for-1 (.000); 1986-87, 0-for-1 (.000); 1987-88 0-for-1 (.000).
Totals: 0-for-5 (.000).

PLAYOFF RECORD

Year	Team	G	Min	FGM	FGA	Pct	FTM	FTA	Pct	Off	Def	Tot	Ast	PF-Dq	St	Bl	Pts	Avg
76-77	G.S.	10	239	52	108	.481	17	26	.654	43	60	103	11	42-1	7	11	121	12.1
80-81	Bos.	17	492	108	219	.493	39	58	.672	50	96	146	19	74-2	21	39	255	15.0
81-82	Bos.	12	426	102	209	.488	51	75	.680	43	92	135	18	47-1	5	48	255	21.3
82-83	Bos.	7	249	43	89	.483	17	20	.850	21	53	74	9	18-0	5	9	103	14.7
83-84	Bos.	23	869	139	291	.478	64	99	.646	76	172	248	27	100-6	23	41	342	14.9
84-85	Bos.	21	803	136	276	.493	87	111	.784	57	162	219	31	68-0	21	34	359	17.1
85-86	Bos.	18	591	106	225	.471	58	89	.652	52	106	158	25	47-1	9	30	270	15.0
86-87	Bos.	21	734	149	263	.567	79	103	.767	59	139	198	28	79-4	18	35	377	18.0
87-88	Bos.	17	626	100	188	.532	50	61	.820	51	117	168	21	42-0	11	19	250	14.7
88-89	Bos.	3	112	20	44	.455	7	9	.778	6	20	26	6	5-0	4	2	47	15.7
89-90	Bos.	5	170	31	54	.574	17	18	.944	23	27	50	13	21-0	5	7	79	15.8
TOTALS:		154	5311	986	1966	.502	486	669	.726	481	1044	1525	208	543-15	129	275	2458	16.0

Three-Point Field Goals: 1986-87, 0-for-1 (.000).

ALL STAR GAME RECORD

Year	Team	Min	FGM	FGA	Pct	FTM	FTA	Pct	Off	Def	Tot	Ast	PF-Dq	St	Bl	Pts	Avg
1981	Bos.	25	5	18	.278	6	6	1.000	6	4	10	2	3-0	0	2	16	16.0
1982	Bos.	20	9	12	.750	3	4	.750	0	7	7	1	2-0	0	2	21	21.0
1983	Bos.	18	5	6	.833	3	4	.750	0	3	3	0	2-0	1	1	13	13.0
1984	Bos.	28	5	11	.455	2	4	.500	4	11	15	2	1-0	3	0	12	12.0
1985	Bos.	10	2	5	.400	0	0	.000	3	3	6	1	0-0	0	0	4	4.0
1986	Bos.	7	0	0	.000	0	2	.000	0	1	1	0	0-0	0	1	0	0.0
1987	Bos.	8	2	3	.667	0	0	.000	0	3	3	0	1-0	0	1	4	4.0
1990	Bos.	21	7	11	.636	0	0	.000	2	2	4	2	4-0	0	1	14	14.0
TOTALS:		137	35	66	.530	14	20	.700	15	34	49	8	13-0	4	8	84	10.5

Three-Point Field Goals: None attempted.

SEASON/CAREER HIGHS

	FGM	FGA	FTM	FTA	REB	AST	ST	BL	PTS
1989-90/Regular Season	15/16	22/31	10/13	12/18	18/32	5/10	3/6	4/9	38/40
1990/Playoffs	10/14	15/25	6/1	16/15	16/19	4/6	2/5	3/7	22/33

JIM PAXSON

Birthdate: July 9, 1957
Birthplace: Kettering, OH
High School: Archbishop Alter (Kettering, OH)
College: Dayton '79
Height: 6-6
Weight: 210
Position: Guard
Years Pro: 11 Years

How Acquired: Traded by Portland to Boston for Jerry Sichting and future considerations on February 23, 1988.

1989-90 Season: In his second full season with Boston, he had 25 starts - the first two games of the season, 20 straight from 11/29-1/12, and the last three of the regular season... 10+ mins 60 times... 20+ mins 27 times... 30+ mins 10 times... 10+ pts 16 times... DNP-CD 10 times... had 30 assists in 5 games, 1/3 thru 1/10... scored 36 points in a 3 game stretch from 3/4-3/9... missed three games from 3/21-3/24 due to a strained left Achilles' tendon suffered on 3/18... in consecutive games on 3/30 and 4/1, he scored 26 pts (8-11, 10-10)... participated in all five playoff games.

Professional Career: Drafted by Portland on the first-round of the 1979 draft, the 12th pick overall... after a rookie year in which he averaged 6.2 points and shot .412 from the floor, he led the Blazers in scoring with 17.7 points a game and .536 from the floor in 1980-81... in 1981-82, he was team captain, and was the only Blazer to start all 82 games; scored in double figures in 80 contests... paced the Blazers in scoring in 1982-83 with a 21.7 average, and in 1983-84 with 21.3... played in the 1983 and 1984 All-Star Games... named to the All-NBA Second Team in 1984... shot a career high .889 at the foul line to rank fourth in the NBA during the 1985-86 season... traded to the Cavs on 6/22/87 for Keith Lee, but the trade was rejected after Lee failed his physical with Portland... had toe surgery in October, 1987, keeping him out of action until January, 1988; surgery was done to remove spurs at the base of his right toe...came to Boston on 2/23/88, and was a key figure off the bench in his initial season with Boston... had a lower back injury in the 1988 playoffs, limiting his play... started seven times at small forward in 1988-89, when Larry Bird was injured... on 3/28/89, Jim underwent surgery to repair torn ligaments in his right wrist; he missed the remainder of the season, as surgery was performed by Dr. Arnold Scheller and Dr. Lewis Millender.

College Career: Averaged 18.0 ppg in 108 career contests, including 23.2 as a senior... was a strong shooter with a career mark of .521, including .546 as a sophomore... scored 1,945 total points... played over 1,000 minutes in each of the first three seasons.

Personal: James Joseph Paxson Jr. is single... his father Jim played with the Minneapolis Lakers (1956-57) and the Cincinnati Royals (1957-58)... most influential person: his father... brother John plays in the NBA... was the Vice-President of the Players Association... enjoys football, baseball, and golf... lists The Rolling Stones, The Police, The Who and David Bowie as some of his favorite rock groups... most memorable Christmas: 1988, because his sons became aware of the holiday spirit... returns to Oregon in the summer... shoe size is 13 and a half.

Career Highs: 41 points vs. Chicago (3-16-84) 11 assists vs. Denver (12-22-85) 8 rebounds at New Jersey (2-20-81)

TOP REGULAR SEASON PERFORMANCES

Points
21 vs. L21 vs. LA Clippers (1-9-89)
20 vs. Golden State (11-16-88)
20 vs. Indiana (1-11-89)
19 at Cleveland (4-15-88)

Rebounds
5 at Washington (4-17-88)
5 vs. Golden State (11-16-88)
4 at Atlanta (11-26-88)
4 at New Jersey (1-9-90)

Assists
9 vs. LA Clippers (1-5-90)
6 at New Jersey (1-9-90)
6 vs. Detroit (1-10-90)
6 vs. Orlando (4-18-90)

NBA RECORD

Year	Team	G	Min	FGM	FGA	Pct	FTM	FTA	Pct	Off	Def	Tot	Ast	PF-Dq	St	Bl	Pts	Avg
79-80	Por.	72	1270	189	460	.411	64	90	.711	25	84	109	144	97-0	48	5	443	6.2
80-81	Por.	79	2701	585	1092	.536	182	248	.734	74	137	211	299	172-1	140	9	1354	17.1
81-82	Por.	82	2756	662	1258	.526	220	287	.767	75	146	221	276	159-0	129	12	1552	18.9
82-83	Por.	81	2740	682	1323	.515	388	478	.812	68	106	174	231	160-0	140	17	1756	21.7
83-84	Por.	81	2686	680	1322	.514	345	410	.841	68	105	173	251	165-0	122	10	1722	21.3
84-85	Por.	68	2253	508	988	.514	196	248	.790	69	153	222	264	115-0	101	5	1218	17.9
85-86	Por.	75	1931	372	792	.470	217	244	.889	42	106	148	278	156-3	94	5	981	13.1
86-87	Por.	72	1798	337	733	.460	174	216	.806	41	98	139	237	134-0	76	12	874	12.1
87-88	Por/Bos	45	801	137	298	.460	68	79	.861	15	30	45	76	73-0	30	5	374	7.7
88-89	Bos.	57	1138	202	445	.454	84	103	.816	18	56	74	107	96-0	38	8	492	8.6
89-90	Bos.	72	1283	191	422	.453	73	90	.811	24	53	77	137	115-0	33	5	460	6.4
TOTALS:		784	21357	4545	9133	.498	2011	2493	.806	519	1074	1593	2300	1442-4	951	93	11199	14.9

Three-Point Field Goals:1979-80, 1-for-22 (.045); 1980-81, 2-for-30 (.067); 1981-82, 8-for-35 (.229); 1982-83, 4-for-25 (.160); 1983-84, 17-for-59 (.288); 1984-85, 6-for-39 (.154); 1985-86, 20-for-62 (.323); 1986-87, 26-for-98 (.265); 1987-88, 5-for-21 (.238); 1988-89, 4-for-24 (.167); 1989-90, 5-for-20 (.250). Totals:98-for-43 (.225).

PLAYOFF RECORD

Year	Team	G	Min	FGM	FGA	Pct	FTM	FTA	Pct	Off	Def	Tot	Ast	PF-Dq	St	Bl	Pts	Avg
79-80	Por.	3	44	5	16	.313	6	6	1.000	0	4	4	3	2-0	2	1	16	5.3
80-81	Por.	1	4	0	3	.000	0	0	.000	0	0	0	0	0-0	0	0	0	0.0
82-83	Por.	7	260	68	11	.586	25	33	.758	4	11	15	18	11-0	9	1	163	23.3
83-84	Por.	5	172	40	78	.513	33	40	.825	11	8	19	12	13-0	2	0	114	22.8
84-85	Por.	9	212	47	101	.465	19	24	.792	6	14	20	21	16-0	6	0	116	12.9
85-86	Por.	4	71	14	37	.378	12	15	.800	1	3	4	15	12-1	3	0	42	10.5
86-87	Por.	4	94	13	32	.406	8	9	.889	4	5	9	13	8-0	5	0	34	8.5
87-88	Bos.	15	188	17	59	.288	16	20	.800	1	8	9	11	18-0	6	2	50	3.3
88-89	Injured																	
89-90	Bos.	5	62	8	16	.500	3	4	.750	0	0	0	7	1-0	5	0	19	3.8
TOTALS		53	1107	212	458	463	122	151	.808	27	53	80	100	81-1	38	4	554	10.5

Three-Point Field Goals:1982-83, 2-for-4 (.500); 1983-84, 1-for-5 (.200); 1984-85, 3-for-10 (.300); 1985-86, 2-for-6 (.333); 1986-87, 0-for-2 (.000); 1987-88, 0-for-2 (.000); 1988-89, 0-for-1 (.000). Totals:8-for-30 (.267).

ALL STAR GAME RECORD

Year	Team	Min	FGM	FGA	Pct	FTM	FTA	Pct	Off	Def	Tot	Ast	PF-Dq	St	SI	Pts	Avg
1983	Por	17	5	7	.714	1	2	.500	0	0	0	1	0-0	2	0	11	11.0
1984	Por.	14	5	9	.556	0	0	.000	1	2	3	2	0-0	0	0	10	10.0
Totals		31	10	16	.625	1	2	.500	1	2	3	3	0-0	2	0	21	11.5

SEASON/CAREER HIGHS

	FGM	FGA	FTM	FTA	REB	AST	ST	BL	PTS
11989-90/Regular Season	8/18	14/33	8/13	8/15	4/8	9/11	3/6	1/2	18/41
1990/Playoffs	4/13	6/21	3/8	3/12	0/6	5/5	3/3	0/2	11/32

ED PINCKNEY

Birthdate: March 27, 1963
Birthplace: Bronx, NY
High School: Adlai Stevenson High (NY)
College: Villanova '85
Height: 6-9
Weight: 215
Position: Forward
Years Pro: 5 years

How Acquired: Traded by Sacramento with Joe Kleine to Boston for Danny Ainge and Brad Lohaus on February 23, 1989.

1989-90 Season: In his first full season with Boston, he was a member of the starting unit 50 times, including the initial 32 games and 18 consecutive from 1/13-2/21... 10+ mins 57 times... 20+ mins 21 times... 30+ mins once... 10+ pts 11 times... DNP- CD 5 times... streak of 22 straight free throws snapped on 12/26... 13 points (6-6, 1-2), with 5 assists at Orlando in 21 minutes on 1/17... had a season high 19 points (6-8, 7-8) vs. Chicago on 4/20... played in four playoff games, and made all 6 shots in Game Two against New York; had 16 points and 4 rebounds in 14 minutes during Boston's record-breaking victory.

Professional Career: Drafted by Phoenix on the first-round of the 1985 draft, the 10th pick overall... played his first two professional seasons with the Suns... traded to the Kings on June 21, 1987, along with a 1988 second-round draft choice in exchange for Eddie Johnson... had seven starts in the 1987-88 season... led the Kings in field goal percentage in 1987-88 (.522)... played 54 games with the Kings in 1988-89, including 24 starts... led Sacramento by shooting 50.2% in 1988-89 before the trade to Boston... started nine times in his initial season with Boston.

College Career: Member of the 1985 NCAA Champions... chosen MVP of the NCAA Division One Tournament in 1985... honorable mention All-America as a sophomore, junior, and senior... led the Wildcats in blocks, rebounds, and fg% all four years... 1983 Gold Medal-winner in the Pan American Games... graduated as Villanova's fifth best scorer (1,865), fourth best rebounder (1,107), and top field goal shooter (.604)... remarkably, his lowest fg% was .568 as a sophomore.

Personal: Edward Lewis Pinckney and his wife Rose have two children, Shea (11/5/84) and Spence (8/22/88)... nicknamed "E-Z Ed" ... has seven sisters... involved in People Reaching Out (PRO), a family counseling center specializing in prevention and intervention of drug and alcohol abuse... favorite television show is "The Fugitive"... favorite NBA city (outside Boston) is New York... likes playing in Madison Square Garden... most influential person: his dad... graduated with a degree in Communications... most memorable Christmas: junior year in college, spending it at Disney World during a basketball tournament in Orlando... lives in New Jersey during the summer... shoe size is 13.

Career Highs: 27 points vs. Seattle (3-26-86) 17 rebounds at Chicago (11-8-86)
6 assists vs. Houston (4-1-87)

TOP REGULAR SEASON PERFORMANCES

Points	Rebounds	Assists
22 vs. San Antonio (3-20-89)	13 at Detroit (3-17-89)	6 at Indiana (3-16-89)
22 vs. Portland (3-29-89)	12 at Indiana (3-16-89)	5 at Detroit (3-17-89)
19 vs. New York (3-24-89)	12 vs. Indiana (11-24-89)	5 at Orlando (1-17-90)
19 vs. Chicago (4-20-89)	11 vs. San Antonio (3-20-89)	4 three times

NBA RECORD

Year	Team	G	Min	FGM	FGA	Pct	FTM	FTA	Pct	Off	Def	Tot	Ast	PF-Dq	St	Bl	Pts	Avg
85-86	Pho.	80	1602	255	457	.558	171	254	.673	95	213	308	90	190-3	71	37	681	8.5
86-87	Pho.	80	2250	290	497	.584	257	348	.739	179	401	580	116	196-1	86	54	837	10.5
87-88	Sac.	79	1177	179	343	.522	133	178	.747	94	136	230	66	118-0	39	32	491	6.2
88-89	Sac/Bos	80	2012	319	622	.513	280	350	.800	166	283	449	118	202-2	83	66	918	11.5
89-90	Bos.	77	1082	135	249	.542	92	119	.773	93	132	225	68	126-1	34	42	362	4.7
TOTALS		396	8123	1178	2168	.543	933	1249	.746	627	1165	1792	458	832-7	313	231	3289	8.3

Three-Point Field Goals: 1985-86, 0-for-2 (.000); 1986-87, 0-for-2 (.000); 1987-88, 0-for-2 (.000); 1988-89, 0-for-6 (.000); 1988-89, 0-for-1 (.000). Totals: 0-for-13 (.000).

PLAYOFF RECORD

Year	Team	G	Min	FGM	FGA	Pct	FTM	FTA	Pct	Off	Def	Tot	Ast	PF-Dq	St	Bl	Pts	Avg
88-89	Bos.	3	112	20	44	.455	7	9	.778	6	20	26	6	5-0	4	2	47	15.7
89-90	Bos.	4	25	6	7	.857	7	9	.778	2	4	6	0	3-0	0	0	19	4.8
TOTALS		7	70	9	19	.474	9	11	.818	4	7	11	1	10-0	1	1	27	3.9

Three-Point Field Goals: None attempted.

SEASON/CAREER HIGHS

	FGM	FGA	FTM	FTA	REB	AST	ST	BL	PTS
1989-90/Regular Season	6/10	10/16	8/12	8/15	12/17	5/6	3/6	3/4	19/27
1990/Playoffs	6/6	6/6	4/4	5/5	4/4	0/1	1/1	1/1	16/16

BRIAN SHAW

Birthdate: March 22, 1966
Birthplace: Oakland, CA
High School: Bishop O'Dowd High (CA)
College: Cal-Santa Barbara '88
Height: 6-6
Weight: 190
Position: Guard
Years Pro: 2 years

How Acquired: Celtics first-round draft choice in 1988... 24th pick overall.

1989-90 Season: Played for Il Messaggero Roma in the A1-Italian League... in 30 regular season games, he averaged 25 points and 9 rebounds, both team highs; his 59 assists tied a team best... played in all 30 of his team's regular season games... was also the team leader in minutes played, fgm, and 3-pt fgm... scored a game high 46 points in a season-ending playoff loss; his team lost 111-103 to Scavolini Pesaro in the third game of their second-round best-of-three series... in the playoffs, he totalled a team high 151 points (39-68, .574 2-pt fgs, 12-31, .387 3-pt fgs, and 37-44, .841 fts) in 6 games; added a team high 56 rebounds, and 5 assists (tied for second best on the team)... was a teammate of LA Clippers' top pick Danny Ferry... announcement of his return to the Celtics was made on February 27, 1990.

Professional Career: Drafted by Boston on the first-round of the 1988 draft, the 24th pick overall... the only Celtic to play in every game in 1988-89... started the last 45 regular season games, and a total of 54 during his rookie season... numbers as a starter: 54 games, 1769 mins, 227-517 (.439) fgs, 0-6 (.000) 3-ptrs, 78-94 (.830) fts, 295 rebs (5.5), 349 assts (6.5), 532 pts (9.9) in 1988-89... 10+ mins 81 times... 20+ mins 68 times... 30+ mins 36 times... 40+ mins 12 times... 10+ rebs 9 times... 10+ assts 12 times... 15 double-doubles... 10+ pts 31 times... 20+ pts twice... 30+ pts once... had the most starts by a Celtics' rookie since Larry Bird in 1979-80, and became the first Celtics' rookie to play in every game since Kevin McHale in 1980-81... the only Celtics' player to register three 40+ minute outputs in the 1989 playoffs... chosen to the NBA All-Rookie Second Team (was the sixth highest point getter among NBA rookies)... signed with the Italian team on August 10, 1989.

College Career: Named the Pacific Coast Athletic Association Player of the Year after his senior season... became the first point guard in PCAA history to lead the conference in rebounding with 9.1 rpg... originally attended St. Mary's (CA) playing in 41 games over two years... sat out 1985-86 as a redshirt... transferred to UCSB and was Second Team All-PCAA in 1986-87... emerged as one of the West Coast's top players in senior season, posting averages of 13.3 ppg, 8.8 rpg and 6.1 apg... became Santa Barbara's all-time leader in assists (375) in 59 games over two seasons... connected on 44 of 116 three-pointers for a .379 accuracy mark in two years at UCSB... helped lead Santa Barbara to an NCAA Tournament appearance.

Personal: Brian K. Shaw is single... lists fishing and playing cards as his hobbies... loves music, especially rap... favorite recreational sports are basketball, football, and baseball... before turning pro, he listed his favorite athletes as Magic Johnson and Charles Barkley... as a youngster, he rooted for the Los Angeles Lakers... returns to California during the summer... favorite food is gumbo... shoe size is 14.

TOP REGULAR SEASON PERFORMANCES

Points
31 at Phoenix (2-17-89)
21 at Denver (12-27-88)
18 three times
17 vs. New Jersey (11-30-88)

Rebounds
15 at Atlanta (4-13-89)
14 at Philadelphia (3-28-89)
12 at Charlotte (4-17-89)
11 three times

Assists
13 at New York (2-26-89)
12 vs. Milw at Htfd (2-24-89)
12 vs. Washntn (4-18-89)
11 two times

NBA AND PRO RECORD

Year	Team	G	Min	FGM	FGA	Pct	FTM	FTA	Pct	Off	Def	Tot	Ast	PF-Dq	St	Bl	Pts	Avg
88-89	Bos.	82	2301	297	686	.433	109	132	.826	119	257	376	472	211-1	78	27	703	8.6
89-90	Roma	30	1144	244	418	.584	111	139	.799	71	203	274	69	NA-NA	80	18	749	25.0

Three-Point Field Goals:1988-89, 0-for-13 (.000); 1989-90, 50-for-140 (.357).
Totals: 0-for-13 (.000).

PLAYOFF RECORD

Year	Team	G	Min	FGM	FGA	Pct	FTM	FTA	Pct	Off	Def	Tot	Ast	PF-Dq	St	Bl	Pts	Avg
88-89	Bos.	3	124	22	43	.512	7	9	.778	2	15	17	19	11-0	3	0	51	17.0
89-90	Roma	6	228	39	68	.574	37	44	.841	13	43	56	5	19-0	9	6	151	25.2

Three-Point Field Goals:1988-89, 0-for-1 (.000); 1989-90, 12-for-31 (.387).
Totals: 0-for-1 (.000).

NOTE: The Italian League compiles two-point field goals and three-point field goals separately, unlike the NBA.

SEASON/CAREER HIGHS

	FGM	FGA	FTM	FTA	REB	AST	ST	BL	PTS
1988-89/Regular Season	14/14	23/23	6/6	6/6	15/15	13/13	7/7	2/2	31/31
1989/Playoffs	8/8	16/16	4/4	4/4	8/8	8/8	2/2	0/0	20/20

CHARLES SMITH

Birthdate: November 29, 1967
Birthplace: Washington, D.C.
High School: All Saints High (Washington, D.C.)
College: Georgetown '89
Height: 6-1
Weight: 160
Position: Guard
Pro Experience: 1 Year

How Acquired: Signed as a free agent on September 25, 1989.

1989-90 Season: After not seeing action in the first three games of his rookie campaign, he played in the next 17, thru 12/9... DNP-CD 22 times... 10+ mins 22 times... 20+ mins 9 times... 30+ mins 3 times... 10+ pts 5 times... had five steals twice... in consecutive games on 2/23 and 2/25, he totalled 59 mins, 11 rebs, 16 assts, 20 pts (7-13, 6-10); played valuable minutes in both wins... vs. Washington, 3/9: 32 mins, 11 pts (5-6, 1-2), 6 rebs and 8 assts... saw action in three of the five playoff contests.

College Career: Winner of Georgetown's "Francis Red Daly" Award as Most Valuable Player after the 1987-88 season... in his junior season, he led the team with a 15.7 scoring average... toured Europe as part of the US Select Team in preparation for the 1988 Olympics... member of 1988 medal-winning Olympic Team... 1988-89 Playboy All-America.

Personal: Charles Edward Smith IV is single... enjoys viewing movies, and shopping... likes all types of food... relaxes to jazz music... most memorable Christmas: all, because of his religious faith... most influential person: his mom... lives in Boston year-round... one of the few professional athletes to wear number 13... shoe size is 10 and a half.

TOP REGULAR SEASON PERFORMANCES

Points
12 at Denver (2-25-90)
11 vs. Wash at Htfd (3-9-90)
11 at Cleveland (11-11-89)
10 two times

Rebounds
7 at Denver (2-25-90)
7 at Philadelphia (4-22-90)
6 vs. Wash at Htfd (3-9-90)
4 at Golden State (2-23-90)

Assists
9 vs. Charlotte (2-7-90)
9 at Golden State (2-23-90)
8 vs. Wash at Htfd (3-9-90)
7 at Denver (2-25-90)

NBA RECORD

Year	Team	G	Min	FGM	FGA	Pct.	FTM	FTA	Pct.	Off	Def	Tot	Ast	PF-Dq	St	Bl	Pts	Avg
89-90	Bos.	60	519	59	133	.444	53	76	.697	14	55	69	103	75-0	35	3	171	2.9

Three-Point Field Goals: 1989-90, 0-for-7 (.000).

PLAYOFF RECORD

89-90	Bos.	3	9	1	2	.500	0	0	.000	1	0	1	3	0-0	1	0	2	0.7

Three-Point Field Goals: None attempted.

SEASON/CAREER HIGHS

	FGM	FGA	FTM	FTA	REB	AST	ST	BL	PTS
1989-90/Regular Season	5/5	12/12	6/6	8/8	7/7	9/9	5/5	1/1	12/12
1990/Playoffs	1/1	1/1	0/0	0/0	1/1	3/3	1/1	0/0	2/2

MICHAEL SMITH

Birthdate: May 19, 1965
Birthplace: Rochester, NY
High School: Los Altos High (Hacienda Heights, CA)
College: Brigham Young '89
Height: 6-10
Weight: 225
Position: Forward
Years Pro: 1 year

How Acquired: Celtics first-round draft choice in 1989... 13th pick overall.

1989-90 Season: Began the season on the injured list with a lower back injury and shin splints... activated on 11/17, saw his first action that night vs. Minnesota... 16 pts/8 assts in 24 mins vs. Kings, on 2/4... free throw breakdown: 1989, 1-for-4, 1990, 52-for-60; began the month of February at .400 (2-for-5)... played in 40 straight games from 1/12-4/4... DNP-CD 9 times ... 10+ mins 24 times... 20+ mins 11 times... 30+ mins 5 times... 10+ pts 13 times... 20+ pts 2 times... 10+ rebs once... one double-double... started 7 straight games from 2/23 thru 3/9; his numbers: 194 mins, 102 pts (44-88, 1-11, 13-16), 27 rebs, and 15 assts... played in four playoff games, made 5 of 8 fgs and all 7 fts... received a vote to the All-Rookie Team.

College Career: Three-time All-WAC First Team selection, averaging 19.0 points over four years... finished as BYU's second all-time leading scorer (2,319 points) behind Danny Ainge... connected on 116-for-270 (.430) three-point attempts in his career and helped lead the Cougars to three consecutive NCAA Tournament appearances... broke conference record for field goals made (previous record was 428 by Devin Durrant)... his career free throw percentage (.878) is the best in conference history... Division One ft% leader in 1988-89, making 160 of 173 shots (.925)... missed the 1984-85 and 1985-86 basketball seasons while serving on a Mormon mission in Argentina.

Personal: Michael John Smith and his wife Michelle have one child, Kenya Michal Smith (11/9/89)... couple married on October 8, 1988... majored in Spanish, and graduated with an impressive grade point average... most influential person: oldest brother Clark Smith... played volleyball and football in high school, and was the recipient of many awards in both sports... extremely intelligent and personable... returns to California during the summer... shoe size is 14.

TOP REGULAR SEASON PERFORMANCES

Points
24 at Denver (2-25-90)
21 vs. Dallas (2-28-90)
17 at Orlando (3-16-90)
17 vs. Orlando (4-18-90)

Rebounds
10 at Miami (3-2-90)
6 at Philadelphia (4-22-90)
5 at Denver (2-25-90)
5 vs. Dallas (2-28-90)
5 at Dallas (3-14-90)

Assists
8 vs. Sacramento (2-4-90)
6 vs. Orlando (4-18-90)
5 at Orlando (3-16-90)
4 at Miami (3-2-90)
4 at Philadelphia (4-22-90)

NBA RECORD

Year	Team	G	Min	FGM	FGA	Pct.	FTM	FTA	Pct.	Off	Def	Tot	Ast	PF-Dq	St	Bl	Pts	Avg
89-90	Bos.	65	620	136	286	.476	53	64	.828	40	60	100	79	51-0	9	1	327	5.0

Three-Point Field Goals: 1989-90, 2-for-28 (.071).

PLAYOFF RECORD

Year	Team	G	Min	FGM	FGA	Pct.	FTM	FTA	Pct.	Off	Def	Tot	Ast	PF-Dq	St	Bl	Pts	Avg
89-90	Bos.	4	16	5	8	.625	7	7	1.000	0	0	0	0	1-0	1	0	17	4.3

Three-Point Field Goals: 1989-90, 0-for-2 (.000).

SEASON/CAREER HIGHS

	FGM	FGA	FTM	FTA	REB	AST	ST	BL	PTS
1989-90/Regular Season	11/11	18/18	5/5	6/6	10/10	8/8	1/1	1/1	24/24
1990/Playoffs	4/4	5/5	4/4	4/4	0/0	0/0	1/1	0/0	9/9

DEE BROWN

Birthdate: November 29, 1968
Birthplace: Jacksonville, FL
High School: Bolles High (FL)
College: Jacksonville '90
Height: 6-1
Weight: 161
Position: Guard
Years Pro: Rookie

How Acquired: Celtics first-round draft choice in 1990... 19th pick overall.

1989-90 Season: Team leader in scoring, assists, steals, minutes and three-point shooting... ranked 10th in the nation in steals with 3.0 per game, and set conference record for steals in a season with 88... set Sun Belt Conference Tournament record with 41 points in quarterfinal game against Old Dominion... named to All-SBC First Team, and to All-Tournament team at Orlando All-Star Classic in April.

College Career: Played 21 games as a freshman, started once... moved into the starting lineup for 23 games as a sophomore, mainly at shooting guard... led Jacksonville in steals (46) and free throw shooting (.818), and ranked second in scoring with 10.1 ppg... named to the All-SBC Second Team as a junior, starting all 30 games; played predominantly at small forward... led the Dolphins in scoring (19.6 ppg), rebounding (7.6 rpg) and steals (56)... started 16 games at point guard and 13 at small forward as a senior as he averaged 19.3 points, 5.0 assists, and 6.6 rebounds per game... finished as ninth all-time scorer in school history with 1,503 points, and finished second behind Ronnie Murphy on all-time steals list with 201... set team record for career three-pointers made with 87... field goal percentage and assists total increased each season... best season statistically was as a junior, as he posted highs in games, free throws made, free throws attempted, free throw percentage, rebounds, points, and points per game.

Personal: Dee Brown in single... nicknamed "Dee-lightful" by his teammates at Jacksonville... a computer whiz, he has owned a computer since the age of eight... has designed his own computer programs... wore number four in college, the same number as his favorite NBA player Ron Harper... lived in Jacksonville his entire life.

COLLEGIATE RECORD

Year	Team	G	FGM	FGA	Pct.	FTM	FTA	Pct.	Rebs	Ast	Pts	Avg
86-87	Jax	21	28	65	.431	13	22	.591	28	17	71	3.4
87-88	Jax	28	108	239	.452	54	66	.818	125	56	282	10.1
88-89	Jax	30	219	447	.490	108	131	.824	228	112	589	19.6
89-90	Jax	29	231	466	.496	69	101	.683	192	151	561	19.3
TOTALS:		108	586	1217	.482	244	320	.763	573	336	1503	13.9

ERIC McARTHUR

Birthdate: August 23, 1968
Birthplace: Pasadena, CA
High School: South Pasadena High (CA)
College: UCSB '90
Height: 6-6
Weight: 195
Position: Forward
Years Pro: Rookie

How Acquired: Signed as a free agent.

1989-90 Season: Started in all 29 of his appearances... was the Gaucho's leading rebounder with 13.0 rpg... finished second at 15.6 ppg to Carrick Dehart's 15.9 ppg... tied or led the team in rebounding in 25 of his 29 games, including both NCAA tourney contests... in UCSB's lone NCAA tourney win (70-66 over Houston), he was the squad's top scorer with 20... recipient of many honors: AP All-America, UPI All-America, The Sporting News All-America Honorable Mention, Hoop Scoop 7th Team All-America, Hoop Scoop All-Sleeper Team, USBWA All-District 8 1st

Team, NABC All-Region 1st Team, Basketball Weekly All-Region Team, Member of NABC All-America Game West Team, West Team Member Hula Classic in Tokyo, Basketball Times All-Region Honorable Mention, Basketball Times All-Rodney Team (No Respect), Street and Smith's Preseason High Honorable Mention All-America, All-Big West 1st Team, three-time Big West Player of the Week, voted best rebounder and interior defender in Big West by coaches, NCAA"s second leading rebounder (13.0), Big West's rebounding and shot blocking champion.

College Career: Four year member of the Gauchos... all-time team leader in total rebounds (904), offensive rebounds (342), free throws attempted (486), and blocked shots (249)... holds season records for rebounds (377), and blocked shots (91)... The Sporting News All-America Honorable Mention in 1989, All-Big West 2nd Team in 1989... three-time Player of the Week in 1989... Big West All-Tournament Team in 1989... All-Tournament Team Amana Hawkeye Classic in 1989... voted best rebounder and interior defender in Big West by coaches in 1989, Big West's rebounding and shot blocking champion in 1989, Kactus Klassic MVP in 1988.

Personal: Eric McArthur is single... is nicknamed The Freeze"... enjoys computers... likes making models, especially airplanes... majored in sociology... parents names are Melvin and Sara... was the fan's favorite in college.

COLLEGE RECORD

Year	Team	G-GS	Min	FGM	FGA	Pct	FTM	FTA	Pct	Off	Def	Rebs	Ast	PF-Dq	St	Bl	Pts	Avg
86-87	UCSB	15-0	78	11	19	.579	7	17	.412	8	19	27	1	16-0	4	16	29	1.9
87-88	UCSB	30-29	653	95	162	.586	66	136	.485	78	118	196	15	99-2	21	64	256	8.5
88-89	UCSB	30-30	845	152	288	.528	92	151	.609	124	180	304	20	111-8	40	78	396	13.2
89-90	UCSB	29-20	875	172	343	.502	109	182	.599	132	245	377	43	100-3	51	91	453	15.6
TOTALS:		104-88	2451	430	812	.530	274	486	.564	342	562	904	79	326-13	116	249	1134	10.9

Three-Point Field Goals: 1987-88, 0-for-1 (.000); 1988-89, 0-for-1 (.000); Totals: 0-for-2 (.000).

DAVE POPSON

Birthdate: May 17, 1964 `
Birthplace: Wilkes-Barre, PA
High School: Bishop O'Reilly (PA)
College: North Carolina '87
Height: 6-10
Weight: 230
NBA Experience: 1 year
Position: Forward
How Acquired: Signed as a free agent.

1989-90 Season: Participated in nine games with the CBA's Albany Patroons... played in 217 minutes, made 47.3% of his fgs (43-91), made all 10 fts, averaged 10.7 ppg (96 total), 55 rebounbs (20 offensive and 35 defensive), 12 assists, 20 personals, 9 turnovers, 15 blocks, and 3 steals... was placed on the suspended reserve list on December 8th (retroactive to the 7th), when he decided to play in Europe.

Professional Career: Was drafted by the Detroit Pistons on the fourth-round of the 1987 draft, the 88th choice overall... played with Monaco (French first division) in 1987 for former UCLA star Bill Sweek, where he shot 53% and led the team in rebounding... signed with the Los Angeles Clippers on November 17th, 1988 and appeared in 10 games; scored 23 points (11-25, 1-2), with 16 rebounds, 6 assists, and 2 blocks in 68 minutes... was waived on December 8, 1988, and was later signed by the Albany Patroons of the CBA... for Albany, he played in 14 games, 300 minutes, scored 154 points (11.0 average), made 69 of 127 field goals (.543), made 16 of 28 free throws (.571), and totalled 85 rebounds (6.1)... appeared in two postseason contests with the Patroons... later became a member of the Miami Heat, on March 22nd, when Pat Cummings was placed on the injured list, signing a 10-day contract... he signed a second 10-day pact on April 2nd, before signing a pact for the remainder of the season on April 13th... with the Heat, he played 7 games and scored 11 points (5-15, 1-2) with 11 rebounds in 38 minutes... signed as a free agent by the Celtics on September 6th, 1989... participated with the Celtics during the 1989 preseason before being waived on October 31, 1989 (the last cut with Scooter Barry).

College Career: Finished as a career 52% field goal shooter in Dean Smith's balanced offensive scheme.

Personal: David Popson lists his father as his greatest influence on his athletic career... lists his favorite foods as anything his mom makes... James Worthy and Michael Jordan are the players he admires the most.

Career Highs: 8 points at Seattle (12-2-88)
4 rebounds three times
2 assists three times

REGULAR SEASON RECORD

Year	Team	G	Min	FGM	FGA	Pct	FTM	FTA	Pct	Off	Def	Tot	Ast	PF-Dq	St	Bl	Pts	Avg
88-89	LAC/Mi	17	106	16	40	.400	2	4	.500	12	15	27	8	17-0	1	3	34	2.0

STOJAN VRANKOVIC

Birthdate: January 22, 1964
Birthplace: Drnis, Yugoslavia
High School: N/A
College: None
Height: 7-2
Weight: 260
Years Pro: Rookie
Position: Center
How Acquired: Signed as a free agent on April 29, 1988.

1989-90 Season: Played for Aris of Thesalonika (Greece)... his team advanced to the European Final Four, where they lost in the semifinals to Barcelona, the team which eventually lost to Dino Radja's Jugoplastika squad in the title game.

Career: Has the potential to be a prominent factor in the NBA due to his size, height, and jumping ability - an incredible 37-inch vertical leap... a great defensive rebounder, is a tremendous intimidator, who can become a force on the defensive end... on offense, he is a good passer with good hands... a member of the 1988 Yugoslavian Olympic Team, he has also been a member of the Yugoslavian National Team since 1985... can run the floor in excellent fashion... would have been a definite first round 1988 draft pick... due to international commitments, he was unavailable to the Celtics for the 1988-89 and 1989-90 seasons... wore number 11 in the McDonald's Basketball Open in Madrid, when his squad played against Boston... played 21 minutes against Boston on 10/21/88 in Madrid, grabbing 4 rebounds and scoring 4 points (2-3 field goals)... came to Boston to see the Celtics-Warriors game on 11/16/88... Vrankovic's occupation in Yugoslavia is a technician.

Personal: Stojan Vrankovic is married, wife's name is Lola... they have two daughters... he has worn uniform number eleven throughout his career.

Stats not available

CHRIS FORD

HEAD COACH

As a player, Chris Ford developed a reputation for intelligence, leadership, and spirited involvement in each game, characteristics descriptive of a future in basketball beyond one's playing days. On June 12, 1990, Ford's day in the limelight came as he was appointed the eleventh Head Coach of the Boston Celtics, and the sixth former Celtics' player to lead the team. Drafted in the second-round (the 17th pick overall by Detroit in 1972), after a distinguished collegiate career at Villanova (he was elected to the Wildcats' Hall of Fame in 1988), Chris spent his first six years in the NBA with the Detroit Pistons. Ford was a valuable contributor to the Motor City squad. He will forever be noted in Pistons' history because of his steal of an inbounds pass and eventual game-winning basket in Game 3 of the Pistons-Bucks mini-series on April 17, 1976.

That was considered the top play in the club's history at that point. In the early stages of his seventh season with the Pistons, Ford was dealt to Boston with a second-round draft pick (Tracy Jackson) for Earl Tatum on October 18, 1978. The Celtics and Ford would have an affiliation of continuous symmetry. He was voted the Most Valuable Player on the 1978-79 team. Then, in 1979, in what was the most impressive one season turnaround recorded by any NBA team, Ford's value to the Celtics became more evident. On October 12, 1979, as the Green Machine hosted the Houston Rockets in what is otherwise known as Larry Bird's first regular season game, Ford converted the NBA's initial three-point goal in the first year of the trifecta. He quietly developed a reputation as one of the league's best three-point bombers, finishing second that season to Seattle's Fred Brown. He eventually became Nate Archibald's backcourt partner throughout the Celtics' successful 1981 championship drive, then called it a career after the 1981-82 season. Christopher Joseph Ford played ten years in the NBA, appeared in 794 regular season games, and averaged 9.2 points.

Number 42 was an excellent three-point shooter, making 37.5% (126-for-336) of his shots. He also saw action in 58 playoff encounters in which he averaged 7.5 points.

When veteran broadcaster Johnny Most was sidelined with an illness during the 1982-83 season, Ford joined the WRKO radio team, adding his adroit commentary. He also did some volunteer coaching with the flourishing Boston College basketball program. After the BC season ended, Chris was offered a job at that school as an Assistant Coach to Gary Williams. However, Ford rejoined the Celtics on June 9, 1983 when K.C. Jones and Red Auerbach offered him a similar position on the professional level. Ford eventually would engage in two world championships within his first three years on the bench. He joined an elite group of Celtics' personnel (Bill Russell, Tom Heinsohn, and Jones) who have earned championship rings as both a player and coach with the 16-time World Champions.

Chris (1/11/49), his wife Kathy, and their four children, Chris (6/25/75), Katie (4/12/78), Anthony (5/13/82), and Michael (12/6/84) live in Lynnfield, Massachusetts during the season. The family makes Margate, New Jersey their home during the summer months.

Don Casey

ASSISTANT COACH

Don Casey joined the Boston Celtics on July 23, 1990 as an assistant coach to Head Coach Chris Ford.

Casey was the former Head Coach at Temple University from 1973-74 through 1981-82, where he compiled an impressive record of 151-94 (.616). The Owls finished first or second in the East Coast Conference in his last seven years, and he posted 20 or more wins three times. He was twice voted East Coast Conference Coach of the Year, and he led Temple to one NCAA postseason tournament and three NIT berths. In 1982-83, Casey joined the NBA ranks as an Assistant Coach to Paul Westhead (Chicago Bulls), then became an assistant to Jim Lynam (Los Angeles Clippers) the following campaign. In 1984- 85, Casey was a head coach in the Italian Professional League, then returned to the NBA's Clippers as an assistant under Don Chaney and Gene Shue for the next three-plus seasons. On January 19, 1989, Casey became the Clippers' Head Coach replacing Shue for the remainder of the 1988-89 season. Casey was subsequently signed for the 1989-90 season as the Clippers' top man on July 13, 1989, and continued in that capacity throughout the season. Casey's Clippers finished at 30-52, sixth place in the Pacific Division. The Clippers announced after the conclusion of the regular season that Casey's contract would not be renewed. He concluded his tenure as Clippers' Head Coach at 41-85.

Casey has developed a reputation in coaching against zone defenses, and has authored a book on the subject entitled *Temple of Zones*.

Casey was born in Collingwood, New Jersey, and attended high school at Catholic High in Camden, NJ. He graduated from Temple University in 1960 (did not play collegiate basketball). Don (6/17/37), his wife Dwynne, and their three children, Lee Ann (22), Michael (20), and Sean (19), maintain homes in San Diego and Marina del Rey, California.

Don Casey (center) watches the action in rookie camp.

Jon Jennings

ASSISTANT COACH

When Chris Ford was appointed Head Coach of the Boston Celtics, one of his first tasks was the completion of his coaching staff. Ford proudly chose Jon Jennings, formerly the teams' Video Coordinator/Scout to one position.

Jennings, a native of Richmond, Indiana, has an impressive resume of basketball experience. While attending Indiana University from 1981-85, Jennings served Head Coach Bob Knight in various roles during his sophomore and junior years.

In 1983, Jennings served as a summer intern with the Indiana Pacers. His duties included ticket sales, public relations, and assisting George Irvine, the club's Vice-President of Basketball Operations. Jennings acquired valuable knowledge in that latter capacity coordinating all college, CBA, and NBA scouting. At the age of 20, Jennings was hired by Irvine, who brought him to Los Angeles to assist in the coaching duties with the Pacers' summer league squad

Upon Irvine's appointment to Indiana's head coaching position, Jennings began to scout and coordinate videos fulltime. Jennings had a bird's-eye view of Pacers' home games, and upon the completion of first-half action, would edit a two-minute tape used in the halftime discussion between players and coaches.

Jennings then joined the NBA Champion Boston Celtics in the summer of 1986, working as the club's initial Video Coordinator.

When Jim Rodgers was chosen the leader of the Green, Jennings responsibilities increased as he scouted Boston's future opponents as well as college players. Jon also assumed the duties of keeping statistical charts, breaking down the opponents offensive and defensive patterns and formulating this information into game plans.

Jennings is an active participant in the Genesis Fund, a provider for the specialized care and treatment of children born with genetic diseases, birth defects, and mental retardation at the National Birth Defects Center.

Jon (10/2/62) is single, and lives in Marblehead, Mass. A devotee of Winston Churchill, Jennings lists his interests as history, politics, reading and painting.

Jon Jennings makes a point.

RECORDS

CELTICS IN NAISMITH MEMORIAL BASKETBALL HALL OF FAME
at Springfield, Massachusetts

IN ORDER OF ELECTION:

Ed Macauley (1960)
Andy Phillip (1961)
John (Honey) Russell (1964)
Walter Brown (1965)
Bill Mokray (1965)
Alvin (Doggie) Julian (1967)
Arnold (Red) Auerbach (1968)
Bob Cousy (1970)
Bill Russell (1974)
Bill Sharman (1975)
Frank Ramsey (1981)
John Havlicek (1983)
Sam Jones (1983)
Tom Heinsohn (1985)
Bob Houbregs (1986)
Pete Maravich (1986)
Clyde Lovellette (1987)
K.C. Jones (1988)
Dave Bing (1989)
Pete Maravich (1989)

RETIRED CELTICS NUMBERS

1 — Walter Brown
2 — Arnold "Red" Auerbach
6 — Bill Russell
10 — Jo Jo White
14 — Bob Cousy
15 — Tom Heinsohn
16 — Tom (Satch) Sanders
17 — John Havlicek
18 — Dave Cowens
     Jim Loscutoff*
19 — Don Nelson
21 — Bill Sharman
22 — Ed Macauley
23 — Frank Ramsey
24 — Sam Jones
25 — K.C. Jones

* Loscutoff's jersey was retired, but number 18 was kept active for Dave Cowens.

CELTICS ON ALL-NBA TEAM
(Selected by the media)

Player	1st Team	2nd Team	3rd Team	Total
Bob Cousy	10	2	0	12
John Havlicek	4	7	0	11
Bill Russell	3	8	0	11
Larry Bird	9	1	0	10
Bill Sharman	4	3	0	7
Ed Macauley	3	1	0	4
Tom Heinsohn	0	4	0	4
Dave Cowens	0	3	0	3
Sam Jones	0	3	0	3
Jo Jo White	0	2	0	2
Kevin McHale	1	0	0	1
Ed Sadowski	1	0	0	1
Nate Archibald	0	1	0	1
Robert Parish	0	1	2	2

INDIVIDUAL AWARDS

NBA EXECUTIVE OF THE YEAR
(Originated in 1972-73;selected by The Sporting News)
1979-80 Red Auerbach

NBA COACH OF THE YEAR
(Originated in 1962-63; selected by the media)
1964-65 Red Auerbach
1972-73 Tom Heinsohn
1979-80 Bill Fitch

NBA MOST VALUABLE PLAYER
(Originated in 1955-56; selected by NBA players)

1956-57	Bob Cousy
1957-58	Bill Russell
1960-61	Bill Russell
1961-62	Bill Russell
1962-63	Bill Russell
1964-65	Bill Russell
1972-73	Dave Cowens
1983-84	Larry Bird
1984-85	Larry Bird
1985-86	Larry Bird

PLAYOFFS' MOST VALUABLE PLAYER
(Originated in 1969; selected by Sport magazine)

1974	John Havlicek
1976	Jo Jo White
1981	Cedric Maxwell
1984	Larry Bird
1986	Larry Bird

CELTICS ON NBA'S 35TH ANNIVERSARY TEAM

(Chosen in 1980 to honor the top performers in the league's first 35 seasons.)

Coach: Arnold (Red) Auerbach

Players: Bob Cousy
John Havlicek
Bill Russell*

* Russell voted the league's greatest all-time player. (In all 11 players were chosen. The other eight: Kareem Abdul-Jabbar, Elgin Baylor, Wilt Chamberlain, Julius Erving, George Mikan, Bob Pettit, Oscar Robertson and Jerry West.)

CELTICS ON NBA'S SILVER ANNIVERSARY TEAM

(Chosen in 1971 to honor the top performers in the league's first 25 seasons.)

Coach: Arnold (Red) Auerbach

Players: Bob Cousy
Bill Russell
Bill Sharman
Sam Jones

(In all 10 players were chosen. The other six: George Mikan, Bob Pettit, Dolph Schayes, Paul Arizin, Bob Davies and Joe Fulks.)

NBA ROOKIE OF THE YEAR

(Originated in 1952-53; selected by the media)

1956-57 Tom Heinsohn
1970-71 Dave Cowens
(shared with Portland's Geoff Petrie)
1979-80 Larry Bird

NBA ALL-DEFENSIVE TEAM

(Originated in 1968-69; selected by the coaches)

1968-69	Bill Russell (1st team)
	John Havlicek (2nd team)
	Tom Sanders (2nd team)
1969-70	John Havlicek (2nd team)
1970-71	John Havlicek (2nd team)
1971-72	John Havlicek (1st team)
	Don Chaney (2nd team)
1972-73	John Havlicek (1st team)
	Don Chaney (2nd team)
	Paul Silas (2nd team)
1973-74	John Havlicek (1st team)
	Don Chaney (2nd team)
1974-75	John Havlicek (1st team)
	Paul Silas (1st team)
	Don Chaney (2nd team)
	Dave Cowens (2nd team)
1975-76	Dave Cowens (1st team)
	John Havlicek (1st team)
	Paul Silas (1st team)
1979-80	Dave Cowens (2nd team)
1981-82	Larry Bird (2nd team)
1982-83	Larry Bird (2nd team)
	Kevin McHale (2nd team)
1983-84	Larry Bird (2nd team)
	Dennis Johnson (2nd team)
1984-85	Dennis Johnson (2nd team)
1985-86	Kevin McHale (1st team)
	Dennis Johnson (2nd team)
1986-87	Kevin McHale (1st team)
	Dennis Johnson (1st team)
1987-88	Kevin McHale (1st team)
1989-90	Kevin McHale (2nd team)
1988-89	Kevin McHale (2nd team)

NBA SIXTH MAN

(Originated in 1982-83; selected by the media)

1983-84 Kevin McHale
1984-85 Kevin McHale
1985-86 Bill Walton

NBA ALL-ROOKIE TEAM

(Originated in 1962-63; selected by the coaches)

1962-63 John Havlicek
1969-70 Jo Jo White
1970-71 Dave Cowens
1979-80 Larry Bird
1980-81 Kevin McHale
1988-89 Brian Shaw (2nd team)

McHale won the Sixth Man Award for two seasons.

BOSTON CELTICS' COACHES

Year	Coach	Regular Season Won	Lost	Playoffs Won	Lost
1946-47	John (Honey) Russell	22	38	—	—
1947-48	John (Honey) Russell	20	28	1	2
1948-49	Alvin (Doggy) Julian	25	35	—	—
1949-50	Alvin (Doggy) Julian	22	46	—	—
1950-51	Arnold (Red) Auerbach	39	30	0	2
1951-52	Arnold (Red) Auerbach	39	27	1	2
1952-53	Arnold (Red) Auerbach	46	25	3	3
1953-54	Arnold (Red) Auerbach	42	30	2	4
1954-55	Arnold (Red) Auerbach	36	36	3	4
1955-56	Arnold (Red) Auerbach	39	33	1	2
*1956-57	Arnold (Red) Auerbach	44	28	7	3
1957-58	Arnold (Red) Auerbach	49	23	6	5
*1958-59	Arnold (Red) Auerbach	52	20	8	3
*1959-60	Arnold (Red) Auerbach	59	16	5	
*1960-61	Arnold (Red) Auerbach	57	22	8	2
*1961-62	Arnold (Red) Auerbach	60	20	8	6
*1962-63	Arnold (Red) Auerbach	58	22	8	5
*1963-64	Arnold (Red) Auerbach	59	21	8	2
*1964-65	Arnold (Red) Auerbach	62	18	8	4
*1965-66	Arnold (Red) Auerbach	54	26	11	6
1966-67	Bill Russell	60	21	4	5
*1967-68	Bill Russell	54	28	12	7
*1968-69	Bill Russell	48	34	12	6
1969-70	Tom Heinsohn	34	48	—	—
1970-71	Tom Heinsohn	44	38	—	—
1971-72	Tom Heinsohn	56	26	5	6
1972-73	Tom Heinsohn	68	14	7	6
*1973-74	Tom Heinsohn	56	26	12	6
1974-75	Tom Heinsohn	60	22	6	5
*1975-76	Tom Heinsohn	54	28	12	6
1976-77	Tom Heinsohn	44	38	5	4
1977-78	Tom Heinsohn	11	23		
	Thomas (Satch) Sanders	21	27	—	—
1978-79	Thomas (Satch) Sanders	12	12		
	Dave Cowens	27	41	—	—
1979-80	Bill Fitch	61	21	5	4
*1980-81	Bill Fitch	62	20	12	5
1981-82	Bill Fitch	63	19	7	5
1982-83	Bill Fitch	56	26	2	5
*1983-84	K.C. Jones	62	20	15	8
1984-85	K.C. Jones	63	19	13	8
*1985-86	K.C. Jones	67	15	15	3
1986-87	K.C. Jones	59	23	13	10
1987-88	K.C. Jones	57	25	9	—
1988-89	Jimmy Rodgers	42	40	0	3
1989-90	Jimmy Rodgers	52	30	2	3
TOTALS	Ten Coaches	2167	1228	259	173

*NBA Championships

COACHING RECORDS
(Boston only)

Coach	Regular Season Record		Playoff Record	
John Russell	42-66	(.389)	1-2	(.333)
Alvin Julian	47-81	(.367)	0-0	(.000)
Red Auerbach	795-397	(.667)	90-58	(.608)
Bill Russell	162-83	(.661)	28-18	(.609)
Tom Heinsohn	427-263	(.619)	47-33	(.588)
Tom Sanders	23-39	(.371)	0-0	(.000)
Dave Cowens	27-41	(.397)	0-0	(.000)
Bill Fitch	242-86	(.738)	26-19	(.578)
K.C. Jones	308-102	(.751)	65-37	(.637)
J. Rodgers	94-70	(.573)	2-6	(.250)
TOTALS	2167-1228	(.638)	259-173	(.600)

CELTICS' OWNERSHIP

1946-1948:	Walter Brown/Boston Garden-Arena Corporation
1948-1950:	Walter Brown
1950-1964:	Walter Brown/Lou Pieri
1964-1965:	Lou Pieri/Marjorie Brown
1965-1968:	Marvin Kratter/National Equities
1968-1969:	Ballantine Brewery
1969-1971:	E. E. (Woody) Erdman/Trans-National Comm.
1971-1972:	Investors' Funding Corporation
1972-1974:	Bob Schmertz/Leisure Technology
1974-1975:	Bob Schmertz/Irv Levin
1975-1978:	Irv Levin
1978-1979:	John Y. Brown/Harry Mangurian Jr.
1979-1983:	Harry Mangurian Jr.
1983-present:	Don Gaston, Paul Dupee, Jr., Alan Cohen

Don Gaston.

Don Gaston and Alan Cohen.

CELTICS' ASSISTANT COACHES

1946-47-1947-48:	Danny Silva
1948-49-1949-50:	Henry McCarthy
1949-50:	Art Spector
1972-73-1976-77:	John Killilea
1977-78:	Tom (Satch) Sanders
1978-79:	Bob MacKinnon
1977-78-1982-83:	K.C. Jones
1980-81-1987-88:	Jimmy Rodgers
1983-90:	Chris Ford
1984-85-1987-88:	Ed Badger
1988-90	Lanny Van Eman
1990-91-present	Don Casey
1990-91-present	Jon P. Jennings

CELTICS' TRAINERS

1946-47-1957-58:	Harvey Cohn
1958-59-1966-67:	Edward (Buddy) LeRoux
1967-68-1970-71:	Joe DeLauri
1971-72-1978-79:	Frank Challant
1979-80-1986-87:	Ray Melchiorre
1987-88-present:	Ed Lacerte

Parish heads into his 15th NBA season.

CELTICS' CAREER LEADERS - REGULAR SEASON

GAMES
1.	John Havlicek	1,270
2.	Bill Russell	963
3.	Bob Cousy	917
4.	Tom Sanders	916
5.	Don Nelson	872
6.	Sam Jones	871
7.	Dave Cowens	726
8.	Jo Jo White	717
9.	Larry Bird	717
10.	Bill Sharman	680

MINUTES
1.	John Havlicek	46,471
2.	Bill Russell	40,726
3.	Bob Cousy	30,131
4.	Dave Cowens	28,551
5.	Larry Bird	27,460
6.	Jo Jo White	26,770
7.	Sam Jones	24,285
8.	Tom Sanders	22,164
9.	Bill Sharman	21,793
10.	Robert Parish	20,882

POINTS
1.	John Havlicek	26,395
2.	Larry Bird	17,783
3.	Bob Cousy	16,955
4.	Sam Jones	15,411
5.	Bill Russell	14,522
6.	Dave Cowens	13,192
7.	Jo Jo White	13,188
8.	Robert Parish	12,870
9.	Bill Sharman	12,287
10.	Tom Heinsohn	12,194

AVERAGE POINTS (3 Yrs. Min.)
1.	Larry Bird	25.0
2.	John Havlicek	20.8
3.	Ed Macauley	18.9
4.	Kevin McHale	18.7
5.	Tom Heinsohn	18.6
6.	Bob Cousy	18.5
7.	Jo Jo White	18.3
8.	Dave Cowens	18.2
9.	Bill Sharman	18.1
10.	Bailey Howell	18.0

FIELD GOALS ATTEMPTED
1.	John Havlicek	23,930
2.	Bob Cousy	16,465
3.	Larry Bird	14,042
4.	Sam Jones	13,745
5.	Bill Russell	12,930
6.	Jo Jo White	12,782
7.	Dave Cowens	12,193
8.	Tom Heinsohn	11,787
9.	Bill Sharman	10,807
10.	Robert Parish	9,500

FREE THROWS ATTEMPTED
1.	John Havlicek	6,589
2.	Bob Cousy	5,753
3.	Bill Russell	5,614
4.	Larry Bird	4,126
5.	Sam Jones	3,572
6.	Ed Macauley	3,518
7.	Cedric Maxwell	3,496
8.	Bill Sharman	3,451
9.	Tom Heinsohn	3,353
10.	Don Nelson	3,296

FREE THROWS MADE
1.	John Havlicek	5,369
2.	Bob Cousy	4,621
3.	Larry Bird	3,647
4.	Bill Russell	3,148
5.	Bill Sharman	3,047
6.	Sam Jones	2,869
7.	Cedric Maxwell	2,738
8.	Ed Macauley	2,724
9.	Tom Heinsohn	2,648
10.	Don Nelson	2,534

FREE THROW PERCENTAGE (1,500 Att.)
1.	Bill Sharman	.883 (3,047-3,451)
2.	Larry Bird	.879 (3,310-3,764)
3.	Larry Siegfried	.855 (1,500-1,755)
4.	Jo Jo White	.833 (1,892-2,270)
5.	John Havlicek	.815 (5,369-6,589)
6.	Frank Ramsey	.804 (2,480-3,083)
7.	Bob Cousy	.803 (4,621-5,753)
8.	Sam Jones	.803 (2,869-3,572)
9.	Nate Archibald	.790 (1,401-1,773)
10.	Tom Heinsohn	.790 (2,648-3,353)

ASSISTS
1.	Bob Cousy	6,945
2.	John Havlicek	6,114
3.	Larry Bird	4,396
4.	Bill Russell	4,100
5.	Jo Jo White	3,686
6.	Dennis Johnson	3,001
7.	K.C. Jones	2,904
8.	Dave Cowens	2,828
9.	Nate Archibald	2,563
10.	Sam Jones	2,209

REBOUNDS
1.	Bill Russell	21,620
2.	Dave Cowens	10,170
3.	John Havlicek	8,007
4.	Robert Parish	7,412
5.	Larry Bird	7,319
6.	Tom Sanders	5,798
7.	Tom Heinsohn	5,749
8.	Kevin McHale	5,227
9.	Bob Cousy	4,781
10.	Don Nelson	4,517

FIELD GOALS MADE
1.	John Havlicek	10,513
2.	Larry Bird	7,058
3.	Sam Jones	6,271
4.	Bob Cousy	6,167
5.	Bill Russell	5,687
6.	Jo Jo White	5,648
7.	Dave Cowens	5,608
8.	Robert Parish	5,253
9.	Tom Heinsohn	4,773
10.	Bill Sharman	4,620

FIELD GOAL PERCENTAGE (2,000 ATT.)
1.	Kevin McHale	.567 (4,396-7,747)
2.	Cedric Maxwell	.559 (2,786-4,984)
3.	Robert Parish	.551 (4,657-8,455)
4.	Rick Robey	.510 (1,144-2,241)
5.	Larry Bird	.503 (7,009-13,938)
6.	Danny Ainge	.490 (2,266-4,621)
7.	Gerald Henderson	.489 (1,467-3,002)
8.	Don Nelson	.484 (3,717-7,672)
9.	Bailey Howell	.480 (2,290-4,766)
10.	Nate Archibald	.469 (1,567-3,338)

PERSONAL FOULS
1.	John Havlicek	3,281
2.	Tom Sanders	3,044
3.	Dave Cowens	2,783
4.	Bill Russell	2,592
5.	Tom Heisnohn	2,454
6.	Bob Cousy	2,231
7.	Frank Ramsey	2,158
8.	Don Nelson	2,094
9.	Don Chaney	1,840
10.	Bill Sharman	4,620

DISQUALIFICATIONS
1.	Tom Sanders	94
2.	Frank Ramsey	87
3.	Dave Cowens	86
4.	Tom Heisnohn	58
5.	Bob Brannum	42
6.	Robert Parish	42
7.	Don Chaney	40
8.	Jim Loscutoff	40
9.	Cedric Maxwell	32

CELTICS' INDIVIDUAL REGULAR-SEASON RECORDS

SCORING

60	Larry Bird vs Atlanta (at New Orleans)	March 12, 1985
56	Kevin McHale vs Detroit	March 3, 1985
53	Larry Bird vs Indiana	March 30, 1983
51	Sam Jones at Detroit	October 29, 1965
50	Larry Bird at Dallas	March 10, 1986
50	Larry Bird vs Atlanta	November 10, 1989
49	Larry Bird vs Washington	January 27, 1988
49	Larry Bird at Phoenix	February 15, 1988
48	Larry Bird vs Houston	March 17, 1985
48	Larry Bird vs Portland	January 27, 1985
48	Larry Bird vs Atlanta	December 9, 1984
47	Larry Bird vs New York	April 12, 1987
47	Larry Bird at Portland	February 14, 1986
47	Larry Bird vs Detroit	November 27, 1985
47	Larry Bird vs Milwaukee	April 12, 1985

FIELD GOALS MADE

22	Larry Bird vs New York	April 12, 1987
22	Larry Bird vs Atlanta (at New Orleans)	March 12, 1985
22	Kevin McHale vs Detroit	March 3, 1985
21	Larry Bird at Portland	February 14, 1986
21	Larry Bird vs Indiana	March 30, 1983
21	Sam Jones at Detroit	October 29, 1965
20	Larry Bird vs Atlanta	December 9, 1984
20	Larry Bird vs Washington	January 27, 1988
20	Danny Ainge vs Phoenix	December 9, 1988

FREE THROWS MADE

20	Nate Archibald vs Chicago	January 16, 1980
19	Cedric Maxwell vs New Jersey	January 14, 1979
19	John Havlicek vs Seattle	February 6, 1970
19	Frank Ramsey at Detroit	December 3, 1957
19	Bill Sharman at Philadelphia	March 8, 1956

ASSISTS

28	Bob Cousy vs Minneapolis	February 27, 1959
23	Nate Archibald vs Denver	February 5, 1982
21	Bob Cousy vs St Louis	December 21, 1960
19	Nate Archibald at San Antonio	October 23, 1979
19	Bob Cousy vs Cincinnati	February 19, 1963
19	Bob Cousy vs Syracuse	November 24, 1956
18	Nate Archibald at Seattle	December 16, 1982
18	Bob Cousy at New York	November 21, 1959
18	Bob Cousy vs New York	January 18, 1953

REBOUNDS

51	Bill Russell vs Syracuse	February 5, 1960
49	Bill Russell vs Philadelphia	November 16, 1957
49	Bill Russell vs Detroit	March 11, 1965
43	Bill Russell vs Los Angeles	January 20, 1963
41	Bill Russell vs Syracuse	February 12, 1958
41	Bill Russell vs San Francisco	March 14, 1965
40	Bill Russell vs Cincinnati	December 12, 1958
40	Bill Russell vs Philadelphia	February 12, 1961

OPPONENTS' INDIVIDUAL REGULAR SEASON RECORDS

SCORING

64	Elgin Baylor, at Minneapolis	November 8, 1959
62	Wilt Chamberlain, Philadelphia at Boston	January 14, 1962
55	Kareem Abdul-Jabbar, at Milwaukee	December 10, 1971
54	Dominique Wilkins, at Atlanta	February 3, 1987

FIELD GOALS MADE

27	Wilt Chamberlain, Philadelphia at Boston	January 14, 1962
25	Elgin Baylor, at Minneapolis	November 8, 1959
25	Wilt Chamberlain, Phil vs Boston at NY	February 23, 1960

FREE THROWS MADE

22	Richie Guerin, New York at Boston	February 11, 1961
20	Kareem Abdul-Jabbar, Milwaukee at Boston	March 8, 1970

ASSISTS

25	Kevin Porter, at Detroit	March 9, 1979
21	Clem Haskins, Chicago at Boston (OT)	December 6, 1969
21	Earvin Johnson, Laker at Boston	December 15, 1989

REBOUNDS

55	Wilt Chamberlain, at Philadelphia	November 24, 1960
43	Wilt Chamberlain, at Philadelphia	March 6, 1965
42	Wilt Chamberlain, at Philadelphia	January 15, 1960
42	Wilt Chamberlain, at Philadelphia	January 14, 1966
42	Wilt Chamberlain, at Los Angeles	March 7, 1969

Bird set the single-game scoring record in 1985.

Kevin McHale scored 56 points against Detroit in 1985.

BOSTON CELTICS YEAR-BY-YEAR

Year	Home	Road	Neutral	Total
1946-47	14-16	8-22		22-38
1947-48	11-13	9-15		20-28
1948-49	17-12	7-20	1-3	25-35
1949-50	12-14	5-28	5-4	22-46
1950-51	26-6	9-22	4-2	39-30
1951-52	22-7	10-19	7-1	39-27
1952-53	21-3	11-18	14-4	46-25
1953-54	16-6	11-19	15-5	42-30
1954-55	20-5	5-22	11-9	36-36
1955-56	20-7	12-15	7-11	39-33
1956-57	27-4	12-19	5-5	44-28
1957-58	25-4	17-13	7-6	49-23
1958-59	26-4	13-15	13-1	52-20
1959-60	25-2	23-9	11-5	59-16
1960-61	21-7	24-11	12-4	57-22
1961-62	23-5	26-12	11-3	60-20
1962-63	25-5	21-16	12-1	58-22
1963-64	26-4	21-17	12-0	59-21
1964-65	27-3	27-11	8-4	62-18
1965-66	26-5	19-18	9-3	54-26
1966-67	27-4	25-11	8-6	60-21
1967-68	28-9	20-16	6-3	54-28
1968-69	24-12	21-19	13-3	48-34
1969-70	16-21	13-27	15-0	34-48
1970-71	25-14	18-22	1-2	44-38
1971-72	32-9	21-16	3-1	56-26
1972-73	33-6	32-8	3-0	68-14
1973-74	26-6	21-18	9-2	56-26
1974-75	28-13	32-9		60-22
1975-76	31-10	23-18		54-28
1976-77	28-13	16-25		44-38
1977-78	24-17	8-33		32-50
1978-79	21-20	8-33		29-53
1979-80	35-6	26-15		61-21
1980-81	35-6	27-14		62-20
1981-82	35-6	28-13		63-19
1982-83	33-8	23-18		56-26
1983-84	33-8	29-12		62-20
1984-85	35-6	28-13		63-19
1985-86	40-1	27-14		67-15
1986-87	39-2	20-21		59-23
1987-88	36-5	21-20		57-25
1988-89	32-9	10-31		42-40
1989-90	30-11	22-19		52-30
TOTALS	1126-343	787-767	202-88	2167-1228

CELTICS YEAR-BY-YEAR PLAYOFF RESULTS

Year	Record	Pct	GB	Place
46-47	22-38	.367	—27	6th

Not in Playoffs

47-48	20-28	.417	—7	3rd

Quarter Finals (Eliminated 1-2)
3/28/48: Chicago 79, @ Boston 72
3/31/48: @ Boston 81, Chicago 77
4/2/48: Chicago 81, @ Boston 74

48-49	25-35	.417	—13	5th

Not in Playoffs

49-50	22-46	.324	—31	6th

Not in Playoffs

50-51	39-30	.565	—2 1/2	2nd

Division Semifinals (Eliminated 0-2)
3/20/51: New York 83, @ Boston 69
3/22/51: @ New York 92, Boston 78 {B}

51-52	39-27	.591	—1	2nd

Division Semifinals (Eliminated 1-2)
3/19/52: @ Boston 105, New York 94
3/23/52: @ New York 101, Boston 97
3/26/52: New York 88, @ Boston 87 (2ot)

52-53	46-25	.648	—1 1/2	3rd

Division Semifinals (Won 2-0)
3/19/53: Boston 87, @ Syracuse 81
3/21/53: @ Boston 111, Syracuse 105 (4ot)
Division Finals (Eliminated 1-3)
3/25/53: @ New York 95, Boston 91
3/26/53: @ Boston 86, New York 70
3/28/53: @ New York 101, Boston 82
3/29/53: New York 82, @ Boston 75

53-54	42-30	.583	—2	2nd

Division Round Robin
3/16/54: Boston 93, @ New York 71
3/17/54: Syracuse 96, @ Boston 95 (ot)
3/20/54: @ Boston 79, New York 78
3/22/54: @ Syracuse 98, Boston 85
Eastern Division Finals (Eliminated 0-2)
3/25/54: @ Syracuse 109, Boston 94
3/27/54: Syracuse 83, @ Boston 76

54-55	36-36	.500	—7	3rd

Division Semifinals (Won 2-1)
3/15/55: @ Boston 122, New York 101
3/16/55: @ New York 102, Boston 95
3/19/55: Boston 116, @ New York 109
Division Finals (Eliminated 1-3)
3/22/55: @ Syracuse 110, Boston 100
3/24/55: @ Syracuse 116, Boston 110
3/26/55: @ Boston 100, Syracuse 97 (ot)
3/27/55: Syracuse 110, @ Boston 94

55-56	39-33	.542	—6	2nd

Division Semifinals (Eliminated 1-2)
3/17/56: @ Boston 110, Syracuse 93
3/19/56: @ Syracuse 101, Boston 98
3/21/56: Syracuse 102, @ Boston 97

56-57	44-28	.611	+6	1st

Division Finals (Won 3-0)
3/21/57: @ Boston 108, Syracuse 90
3/23/57: Boston 120, @ Syracuse 105
3/24/57: @ Boston 83, Syracuse 80
Championship Finals (Won 4-3)
3/30/57: St. Louis 125, @ Boston 123 (ot)
3/31/57: @ Boston 119, St. Louis 99
4/6/57: @ St. Louis 100, Boston 98
4/7/57: Boston 123, @ St. Louis 118
4/9/57: @ Boston 124, St. Louis 109
4/11/57: @ St. Louis 96, Boston 94
4/13/57: @ Boston 125, St. Louis 123 (2ot) 57-

57-58	49-23	.681	+8	1st

Division Finals (Won 4-1)
3/19/58: @ Boston 107, Philadelphia 98
3/22/58: Boston 109, @ Philadelphia 87
3/23/58: @ Boston 106, Philadelphia 92
3/26/58: @ Philadelphia 111, Boston 97
3/27/58: @ Boston 93, Philadelphia 88
Championship Finals (Eliminated 2-4)
3/29/58: St. Louis 104, @ Boston 102
3/30/58: @ Boston 136, St. Louis 112
4/2/58: @ St. Louis 111, Boston 108
4/5/58: Boston 109, @ St. Louis 98
4/9/58: St. Louis 102, @ Boston 100
4/12/58: @ St. Louis 110, Boston 109

58-59	52-20	.722	+12	1st

Division Finals (Won 4-3)
3/18/59: @ Boston 131, Syracuse 109
3/21/59: @ Syracuse 120, Boston 118
3/22/59: @ Boston 133, Syracuse 111
3/25/59: @ Syracuse 119, Boston 107
3/28/59: @ Boston 129, Syracuse 108
3/29/59: Syracuse 133, Boston 121
4/1/59: @ Boston 130, Syracuse 125
Championship Finals (Won 4-0)
4/4/59: @ Boston 118, Minneapolis 115
4/5/59: @ Boston 128, Minneapolis 108
4/7/59: Boston 123, @ Minneapolis 110
4/9/59: Boston 118, @ Minneapolis 113 {B}

59-60	59-16	.787	+10	1st

Division Finals (Won 4-2)
3/16/60: @ Boston 111, Philadelphia 105
3/18/60: @ Philadelphia 115, Boston 110
3/19/60: @ Boston 120, Philadelphia 90
3/20/60: Boston 112, @ Philadelphia 104
3/22/60: Philadelphia 128, @ Boston 107
3/24/60: Boston 119, @ Philadelphia 117
Championship Finals (Won 4-3)
3/27/60: @ Boston 140, St. Louis 122
3/29/60: St. Louis 113, @ Boston 103
4/2/60: Boston 102, @ St. Louis 86
4/3/60: @ St. Louis 106, Boston 96
4/5/60: @ Boston 127, St. Louis 102
4/7/60: @ St. Louis 105, Boston 102
4/9/60: @ Boston 122, St. Louis 103

60-61	}57-22	.722	+11	1st

Division Finals (Won 4-1)
3/19/61: @ Boston 128, Syracuse 115
3/21/61: @ Syracuse 115, Boston 98
3/23/61: @ Boston 133, Syracuse 110
3/25/61: Boston 120, @ Syracuse 107
3/26/61: @ Boston 123, Syracuse 101

Championship Finals (Won 4-1)
4/2/61: @ Boston 129, St. Louis 95
4/5/61: @ Boston 116, St. Louis 108
4/8/61: @ St. Louis 124, Boston 120
4/9/61: Boston 119, @ St. Louis 104
4/11/61: @ Boston 121, St. Louis 112

61-62	60-20	.750	+11	1st

Division Finals (Won 4-3)
3/24/62: @ Boston 117, Philadelphia 89
3/27/62: @ Philadelphia 113, Boston 106
3/28/62: @ Boston 129, Philadelphia 114
3/31/62: @ Philadelphia 110, Boston 106
4/1/62: @ Boston 119, Philadelphia 104
4/3/62: @ Philadelphia 109, Boston 99
4/5/62: @ Boston 109, Philadelphia 107
Championship Finals (Won 4-3)
4/7/62: @ Boston 122, Los Angeles 108
4/8/62: Los Angeles 129, @ Boston 122
4/10/62: @ Los Angeles 117, Boston 115
4/11/62: Boston 115, @ Los Angeles 103
4/14/62: Los Angeles 126, @ Boston 121
4/16/62: Boston 119, @ Los Angeles 105
4/18/62: @ Boston 110, Los Angeles 107

62-63	58-22	.725	+10	1st

Division Finals (Won 4-3)
3/28/63: Cincinnati 135, @ Boston 132
3/29/63: Boston 125, @ Cincinnati 102
3/31/63: Cincinnati 121, @ Boston 116
4/3/63: Boston 128, @ Cincinnati 110
4/6/63: @ Boston 125, Cincinnati 110
4/7/63: @ Cincinnati 109, Boston 99
4/10/63: @ Boston 142, Cincinnati 131
Championship Finals (Won 4-2)
4/14/63: @ Boston 117, Los Angeles 114
4/16/63: @ Boston 113, Los Angeles 106
4/17/63: @ Los Angeles 119, Boston 99
4/19/63: Boston 108, @ Los Angeles 105
4/21/63: Los Angeles 126, @ Boston 119
4/24/63: Boston 112, @ Los Angeles 109

63-64	59-21	.738	+4	1st

Division Finals (Won 4-1)
3/31/64: @ Boston 103, Cincinnati 87
4/2/64: @ Boston 101, Cincinnati 90
4/5/64: Boston 102, @ Cincinnati 92
4/7/64: @ Cincinnati 102, Boston 93
4/9/64: @ Boston 109, Cincinnati 95
Championship Finals (Won 4-1)
4/18/64: @ Boston 108, San Francisco 96
4/20/64: @ Boston 124, San Francisco 101
4/22/64: @ San Francisco 115, Boston 91
4/24/64: Boston 98, @ San Francisco 95
4/26/64: @ Boston 105, San Francisco 99

64-65	62-18	.755	+14	1st

Division Finals (Won 4-3)
4/4/65: @ Boston 108, Philadelphia 98
4/6/65: @ Philadelphia 109, Boston 103
4/8/65: @ Boston 112, Philadelphia 94
4/9/65: @ Philadelphia 134, Boston 131
4/11/65: @ Boston 114, Philadelphia 108
4/13/65: @ Philadelphia 112, Boston 106
4/15/65: @ Boston 110, Philadelphia 109
Championship Finals (Won 4-1)

4/18/65: @ Boston 142, Los Angeles 110
4/19/65: @ Boston 129, Los Angeles 123
4/21/65: @ Los Angeles 126, Boston 105
4/23/65: Boston 112, @ Los Angeles 99
4/25/65: @ Boston 129, Los Angeles 96

65-66   54-26   .675   —1   2nd
Division Semifinals (Won 3-2)
3/23/66: Cincinnati 107, @ Boston 103
3/26/66: Boston 132, @ Cincinnati 125
3/27/66: Cincinnati 113, @ Boston 107
3/30/66: Boston 120, @ Cincinnati 103
4/1/66: @ Boston 112, Cincinnati 103
Division Finals (Won 4-1)
4/3/66: Boston 115, @ Philadelphia 96
4/6/66: @ Boston 114, Philadelphia 93
4/7/66: @ Philadelphia 111, Boston 105
4/10/66: @ Boston 114, Philadelphia 108 (ot)
4/12/66: Boston 120, @ Philadelphia 112
Championship Finals (Won 4-3)
4/17/66: Los Angeles 133, @ Boston 129 (ot)
4/19/66: @ Boston 129, Los Angeles 109
4/20/66: Boston 120, @ Los Angeles 106
4/22/66: Boston 122, @ Los Angeles 117
4/24/66: Los Angeles 121, @ Boston 117
4/26/66: @ Los Angeles 123, Boston 115
4/28/66: @ Boston 95, Los Angeles 93

66-67   60-21   .741   —8   2nd
Division Semifinals (Won 3-1)
3/21/67: @ Boston 140, New York 110
3/25/67: Boston 115, @ New York 108
3/26/67: New York 123, @ Boston 112
3/28/67: Boston 118, @ New York 109
Division Finals (Eliminated 1-4)
3/31/67: @ Philadelphia 127, Boston 113
4/2/67: Philadelphia 107, @ Boston 102
4/5/67: @ Philadelphia 115, Boston 104
4/9/67: @ Boston 121, Philadelphia 117
4/11/67: @ Philadelphia 140, Boston 116

67-68   54-28   .659   —8   2nd
Division Semifinals (Won 4-2)
3/24/68: @ Boston 123, Detroit 116
3/25/68: @ Detroit 126, Boston 116
3/27/68: Detroit 109, @ Boston 98
3/28/68: Boston 135, @ Detroit 110
3/31/68: @ Boston 110, Detroit 96
4/1/68: Boston 111, @ Detroit 103
Division Finals (Won 4-3)
4/5/68: Boston 127, @ Philadelphia 118
4/10/68: Philadelphia 115, @ Boston 106
4/11/68: @ Philadelphia 122, Boston 114
4/14/68: Philadelphia 110, @ Boston 105
4/15/68: Boston 122, @ Philadelphia 104
4/17/68: @ Boston 114, Philadelphia 106
4/19/68: Boston 100, @ Philadelphia 96
Championship Finals (Won 4-2)
4/10/68: Philadelphia 115, Boston 106
4/21/68: @ Boston 107, Los Angeles 101
4/24/68: Los Angeles 123, @ Boston 113
4/26/68: Boston 127, @ Los Angeles 119
4/28/68: @ Los Angeles 119, Boston 105
4/30/68: @ Boston 120, Los Angeles 117 (ot)
5/2/68: Boston 124, @ Los Angeles 109

68-69   48-34   .585   —9   4th
Division Semifinals (Won 4-1)
3/26/69: Boston 114, @ Philadelphia 100

3/28/69: @ Boston 134, Philadelphia 103
3/30/69: Boston 125, @ Philadelphia 118
4/1/69: Philadelphia 119, @ Boston 116
4/4/69: Boston 93, @ Philadelphia 90
Division Finals (Won 4-2)
4/6/69: Boston 108, @ New York 100
4/9/69: @ Boston 112, New York 97
4/10/69: @ New York 101, Boston 91
4/13/69: @ Boston 97, New York 96
4/14/69: @ New York 112, Boston 104
4/18/69: @ Boston 106, New York 105
Championship Finals (Won 4-3)
4/23/69: @ Los Angeles 120, Boston 118
4/25/69: @ Los Angeles 118, Boston 112
4/27/69: @ Boston 111, Los Angeles 105
4/29/69: @ Boston 89, Los Angeles 88
5/1/69: @ Los Angeles 117, Boston 104
5/3/69: @ Boston 99, Los Angeles 90
5/5/69: Boston 108, @ Los Angeles 106

69-70   34-48   .415   —26   6th
Not in Playoffs

70-71   44-38   .537   —8   3rd
Not in Playoffs

71-72   56-26   .683   +8   1st
Conference Semifinals (Won 4-2)
3/29/72: @ Boston 126, Atlanta 108
3/31/72: @ Atlanta 113, Boston 104
4/2/72: @ Boston 136, Atlanta 113
4/4/72: @ Atlanta 112, Boston 110
4/7/72: @ Boston 124, Atlanta 114
4/9/72: Boston 127, @ Atlanta 118
Conference Finals (Eliminated 1-4)
4/13/72: New York 116, @ Boston 94
4/16/72: @ New York 106, Boston 105
4/19/72: @ Boston 115, New York 109
4/21/72: @ New York 116, Boston 98
4/23/72: New York 111, @ Boston 103

72-73   68-14   .829   +11   1st
Conference Semifinals (Won 4-2)
4/1/73: @ Boston 134, Atlanta 109
4/4/73: Boston 126, @ Atlanta 113
4/6/73: Atlanta 118, @ Boston 105
4/8/73: @ Atlanta 97, Boston 94
4/11/73: @ Boston 108, Atlanta 101
4/13/73: Boston 121, @ Atlanta 103
Conference Finals (Eliminated 3-4)
4/15/73: @ Boston 134, New York 108
4/18/73: @ New York 129, Boston 96
4/20/73: New York 98, @ Boston 91
4/22/73: @ New York 117, Boston 110 (2ot)
4/25/73: @ Boston 98, New York 97
4/27/73: Boston 110, @ New York 100
4/29/73: New York 94, @ Boston 78

73-74   56-26   .683   +7   1st
Conference Semifinals (Won 4-2)
3/30/74: @ Boston 107, Buffalo 97
4/2/74: @ Buffalo 115, Boston 105
4/3/74: @ Boston 120, Buffalo 107
4/6/74: @ Buffalo 104, Boston 102
4/9/74: @ Boston 100, Buffalo 97
4/12/74: Boston 106, @ Buffalo 104
Conference Finals (Won 4-1)
4/14/74: @ Boston 113, New York 88
4/16/74: @ Boston 111, New York 99

4/19/74: New York 103, @ Boston 100
4/21/74: Boston 98, @ New York 91
4/24/74: @ Boston 105, New York 94
Championship Finals (Won 4-3)
4/28/74: Boston 98, @ Milwaukee 83
4/30/74: @ Milwaukee 105, Boston 96 (ot)
5/3/74: @ Boston 95, Milwaukee 83
5/5/74: Milwaukee 97, @ Boston 89
5/7/74: Boston 96, @ Milwaukee 87
5/10/74: Milwaukee 102, @ Boston 101 (2ot)
5/12/74: Boston 102, @ Milwaukee 87

74-75   60-22   .732   +11   1st
Conference Semifinals (Won 4-1)
4/14/75: @ Boston 123, Houston 106
4/16/75: @ Boston 112, Houston 100
4/19/75: @ Houston 117, Boston 102
4/22/75: Boston 122, @ Houston 117
4/24/75: @ Boston 128, Houston 115 Ê
Conference Finals (Eliminated 2-4)
4/27/75: Washington 100, @ Boston 95
4/30/75: @ Washington 117, Boston 92
5/3/75: @ Boston 101, Washington 90
5/7/75: @ Washington 119, Boston 108
5/9/75: @ Boston 103, Washington 99
5/11/75: @ Washington 98, Boston 92

75-76   54-28   .659   +8   1st
Conference Semifinals (Won 4-2)
4/21/76: @ Boston 107, Buffalo 98
4/23/76: @ Boston 101, Buffalo 96
4/25/76: @ Buffalo 98, Boston 93
4/28/76: @ Buffalo 124, Boston 122
4/30/76: @ Boston 99, Buffalo 88
5/2/76: Boston 104, @ Buffalo 100
Conference Finals (Won 4-2)
5/6/76: @ Boston 111, Cleveland 99
5/9/76: @ Boston 94, Cleveland 89
5/11/76: @ Cleveland 83, Boston 78
5/14/76: @ Cleveland 106, Boston 87
5/16/76: @ Boston 99, Cleveland 94
5/18/76: Boston 94, @ Cleveland 87
Championship Finals (Won 4-2)
5/23/76: @ Boston 98, Phoenix 87
5/27/76: @ Boston 105, Phoenix 90
5/30/76: @ Phoenix 105, Boston 98
6/2/76: @ Phoenix 109, Boston 107
6/4/76: @ Boston 128, Phoenix 126 (3ot)
6/6/76: Boston 87, @ Phoenix 80

76-77   44-38   .537   —6   2nd
Eastern Conference First Round (Won 2-0)
4/12/77: @ Boston 104, San Antonio 94
4/15/77: Boston 113, @ San Antonio 109
Eastern Conference Semifinals (Eliminated 3-4)
4/17/77: Boston 113, @ Philadelphia 111
4/20/77: @ Philadelphia 113, Boston 101
4/22/77: Philadelphia 109, @ Boston 100
4/24/77: @ Boston 124, Philadelphia 119
4/27/77: @ Philadelphia 110, Boston 91
4/29/77: @ Boston 113, Philadelphia 108
5/1/77: @ Philadelphia 83, Boston 77

77-78   32-50   .390   —23   3rd
Not in Playoffs

78-79   29-53   .354   —25   5th
Not in Playoffs

79-80   61-21   .744   +2   1st
Conference Semifinals (Won 4-0)
4/9/80:   @ Boston 119, Houston 101
4/11/80: @ Boston 95, Houston 75
4/13/80: Boston 100, @ Houston 81
4/14/80: Boston 138, @ Houston 121
Conference Finals (Eliminated 1-4)
4/18/80: Philadelphia 96, @ Boston 93
4/20/80: @ Boston 96, Philadelphia 90
4/23/80: @ Philadelphia 99, Boston 97
4/25/80: @ Philadelphia 102, Boston 90
4/27/80: Philadelphia 105, @ Boston 94

80-81   62-20   .756   tie   1st
Conference Semifinals (Won 4-0)
4/5/81:   @ Boston 121, Chicago 109
4/7/81:   @ Boston 106, Chicago 97
4/10/81: Boston 113, @ Chicago 107
4/12/81: Boston 109, @ Chicago 103
Conference Finals (Won 4-3)
4/21/81: Philadelphia 105, @ Boston 104
/22/81:   @ Boston 118, Philadelphia 99
4/24/81: @ Philadelphia 110, Boston 100
4/26/81: @ Philadelphia 107, Boston 105
4/29/81: @ Boston 111, @ Philadelphia 109
5/1/81:   Boston 100, @ Philadelphia 98
5/3/81:   @ Boston 91, Philadelphia 90
Championship Finals (Won 4-2)
5/5/81:   @ Boston 98, Houston 95
5/7/81:   Houston 92, @ Boston 90
5/9/81:   Boston 94, @ Houston 71
5/10/81: @ Houston 91, Boston 86
5/12/81: @ Boston 109, Houston 80
5/14/81: Boston 102, @ Houston 91

81-82   63-19   .768   +5   1st
Conference Semifinals (Won 4-1)
4/25/82: @ Boston 109, Washington 91
4/28/82: Washington 103, @ Boston 102
5/1/82:   Boston 92, @ Washington 83
5/2/82:   Boston 103, @ Washington 99 (ot)
5/5/82:   @ Boston 131, Washington 126 (2ot)
Conference Finals (Eliminated 3-4)
5/9/82:   @ Boston 121, Philadelphia 81
5/12/82: Philadelphia 121, @ Boston 113
5/15/82: @ Philadelphia 99, Boston 97
5/16/82: @ Philadelphia 119, Boston 94
5/19/82: @ Boston 114, Philadelphia 85
5/21/82: Boston 88, @ Philadelphia 75
5/23/82: Philadelphia 120, @ Boston 106

82-83   56-26   .683   —9   2nd
Eastern Conference First Round (Won 2-1)
4/19/83: @ Boston 103, Atlanta 95
4/22/83: @ Atlanta 95, Boston 93
4/24/83: @ Boston 98, Atlanta 79
Eastern Conference Semifinals (Eliminated 0-4)
4/27/83: Milwaukee 116, @ Boston 95
4/29/83: Milwaukee 95, @ Boston 91
5/1/83:   @ Milwaukee 107, Boston 99
5/2/83:   @ Milwaukee 107, Boston 93

83-84   62-20   .756   +10   1st
Eastern Conference First Round (Won 3-1)
4/17/84: @ Boston 91, Washington 83
4/19/84: @ Boston 88, Washington 85
4/21/84: @ Washington 111, Boston 108 (ot)
4/24/84: Boston 99, @ Washington 96
Eastern Conference Semifinals (Won 4-3)

4/29/84: @ Boston 110, New York 92
5/2/84:   @ Boston 116, New York 102
5/4/84:   @ New York 100, Boston 92
5/6/84:   @ New York 118, Boston 113
5/9/84:   @ Boston 121, New York 99
5/11/84: @ New York 106, Boston 104
5/13/84: @ Boston 121, New York 104
Eastern Conference Championship (Won 4-1)
5/15/84: @ Boston 119, Milwaukee 96
5/17/84: @ Boston 125, Milwaukee 110
5/19/84: Boston 109, @ Milwaukee 100
5/21/84: @ Milwaukee 122, Boston 113
5/23/84: @ Boston 115, Milwaukee 108
NBA World Championship Series (Won 4-3)
5/27/84: Los Angeles 115, @ Boston 109
5/31/84: @ Boston 124, Los Angeles 121 (ot)
6/3/84:   @ Los Angeles 137, Boston 104
6/6/84:   Boston 129, @ Los Angeles 125 (ot)
6/8/84:   @ Boston 121, Los Angeles 103
6/10/84: @ Los Angeles 119, Boston 108
6/12/84: @ Boston 111, Los Angeles 102

84-85   63-19   .768   +5   1st
Eastern Conference First Round (Won 3-1)
4/18/85: @ Boston 126, Cleveland 123
4/20/85: @ Boston 108, Cleveland 106
4/23/85: @ Cleveland 105, Boston 98
4/25/85: Boston 117, @ Cleveland 115
Eastern Conference Semifinals (Won 4-2)
4/28/85: @ Boston 133, Detroit 99
4/30/85: @ Boston 121, Detroit 114
5/2/85:   @ Detroit 125, Boston 117
5/5/85:   @ Detroit 102, Boston 99
5/8/85:   @ Boston 130, Detroit 123
5/10/85: Boston 123, @ Detroit 113
Eastern Conference Championship (Won 4-1)
5/12/85: @ Boston 108, Philadelphia 93
5/14/85: @ Boston 106, Philadelphia 98
5/18/85: Boston 105, @ Philadelphia 94
5/19/85: @ Philadelphia 115, Boston 104
5/22/85: @ Boston 102, Philadelphia 100
NBA World Championship Series (Lost 2-4)
5/27/85: @ Boston 148, Los Angeles 114
5/30/85: Los Angeles 109, @ Boston 102
6/2/85:   @ Los Angeles 136, Boston 111
6/5/85:   Boston 107, @ Los Angeles 105
6/7/85:   @ Los Angeles 120, Boston 111
6/9/85:   Los Angeles 111, @ Boston 100

85-86   67-15   .817   +13   1st
Eastern Conference First Round (Won 3-0)
4/17/86: @ Boston 123, Chicago 104
4/20/86: @ Boston 135, Chicago 131 (2ot)
4/22/86: Boston 122, @ Chicago 104
Eastern Conference Semifinals (Won 4-1)
4/27/86: @ Boston 103, Atlanta 91
4/29/86: @ Boston 119, Atlanta 108
5/2/86:   Boston 111, @ Atlanta 107
5/4/86:   @ Atlanta 106, Boston 94
5/6/86:   @ Boston 132, Atlanta 99
Eastern Conference Finals (Won 4-0)
5/13/86: @ Boston 128, Milwaukee 96
5/15/86: @ Boston 122, Milwaukee 111
5/17/86: Boston 111, @ Milwaukee 107
5/18/86: Boston 111, @ Milwaukee 98
NBA Finals (Won 4-2)
5/26/86: @ Boston 112, Houston 100
5/29/86: @ Boston 117, Houston 95
6/1/86:   @ Houston 106, Boston 104

6/3/86:   Boston 106, @ Houston 103
6/5/86:   @ Houston 111, Boston 96
6/8/86:   @ Boston 114, Houston 97

86-87   59-23   .720   +14   1st
Eastern Conference First Round (Won 3-0)
4/23/87   @ Boston 108, Chicago 104
4/26/87   @ Boston 105, Chicago 96
4/28/87   Boston 105, @ Chicago 94
Eastern Conference Semifinals (Won 4-3)
5/5/87   @ Boston 111, Milwaukee 98
5/6/87   @ Boston 126, Milwaukee 124
5/8/87   @ Milwaukee 126, Boston 121 (ot)
5/10/87   Boston 138, @ Milwaukee 137 (2ot)
5/13/87   Milwaukee 129, @ Boston 124
5/15/87   @ Milwaukee 121, Boston 111
5/17/87   @ Boston 119, Milwaukee 113
Eastern Conference Finals (Won 4-3)
5/19/87   @ Boston 104, Detroit 91
5/21/87   @ Boston 110, Detroit 101
5/23/87   @ Detroit 122, Boston 104
5/24/87   @ Detroit 145, Boston 119
5/26/87   @ Boston 108, Detroit 107
5/28/87   @ Detroit 113, Boston 105
5/30/87   @ Boston 117, Detroit 114
NBA Finals (Lost 2-4)
6/2/87   @ Los Angeles 126, Boston 113
6/4/87   @ Los Angeles 141, Boston 122
6/7/87   @ Boston 109, Los Angeles 103
6/9/87   Los Angeles 107, @ Boston 106
6/11/87   @ Boston 123, Los Angeles 108
6/14/87   @ Los Angeles 106, Boston 93

87-88   57-25   .695   +19   1st
Eastern Conference First Round (Won 3-1)
4/29/88: @ Boston 112, New York 92
5/1/88:   @ Boston 128, New York 102
5/4/88:   @ New York 109, Boston 100
5/6/88:   Boston 102, New York 94
Eastern Conference Semifinals (Won 4-3)
5/11/88: @ Boston 110, Atlanta 101
5/13/88: @ Boston 108, Atlanta 97
5/15/88: @ Atlanta 110, Boston 92
5/16/88: @ Atlanta 118, Boston 109
5/18/88: Atlanta 112, @ Boston 104
5/20/88: Boston 102, @ Atlanta 100
5/22/88: @ Boston 118, Atlanta 116
Eastern Conference Finals (Lost 2-4)
5/25/88: Detroit 104, @ Boston 96
5/26/88: @ Boston 119, Detroit 115 (2ot)
5/28/88: @ Detroit 98, Boston 94
5/30/88: Boston 79, @ Detroit 78
6/1/88:   Detroit 102, @ Boston 96 (ot)
6/3/88:   @ Detroit 95, Boston 90

88-89   42-40   .512   -10   3rd
Eastern Conference First Round (Lost 0-3)
4/28/89: @ Detroit 101, Boston 91
4/30/89: @ Detroit 102, Boston 95
5/2/89:   Detroit 100, @ Boston 85

89-90   52-30   .634   -1   2nd
Eastern Conference First Round (Lost 2-3)
4/26/90: @ Boston116, New York 105
4/28/90: @ Boston157, New York 128
5/2/90:   @ New York 102, Boston 99
5/4/90:   @ New York 135, Boston 108
5/6/90:   @ New York 121, Boston 114

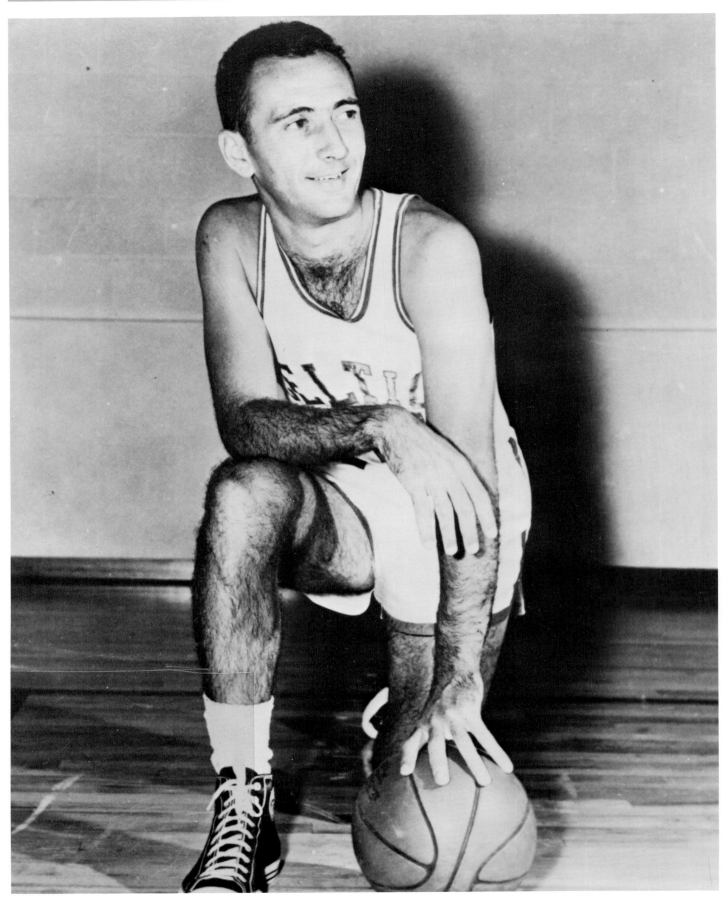

Hall of Famer Bob Cousy.

INDIVIDUAL PLAYOFF RECORDS

MOST POINTS
—Game	54	John Havlicek vs. Atlanta	April 1, 1973
—Half	30	Larry Bird vs. Detroit	April 30, 1985
		John Havlicek vs. Atlanta	April 1, 1973
—Quarter	24	Larry Bird vs. Atlanta	May 11, 1988
—Overtime	12	Bob Cousy at Syracuse	March 17, 1954

MOST FIELD GOALS MADE
—Game	24	John Havlicek vs. Atlanta	April 1, 1973
—Half	14	John Havlicek vs. Atlanta	April 1, 1973
—Quarter	10	Larry Bird vs. Atlanta	May 11, 1988

MOST FIELD GOALS ATTEMPTED
—Game	36	John Havlicek vs. Atlanta	April 1, 1973
—Half	21	Larry Bird vs. Detroit	May 8, 1985
—Quarter	13	Dave Cowens vs. Buffalo	March 30, 1974

MOST FREE THROWS MADE
—Game	30	Bob Cousy vs. Syracuse	March 21, 1953
—Half	12	Larry Bird vs. Detroit	April 30, 1985
—Quarter	9	Frank Ramsey vs. Minneapolis	April 4, 1959

MOST FREE THROWS ATTEMPTED
—Game	32	Bob Cousy vs. Syracuse	March 21, 1953
—Half	15	Bill Russell vs. St. Louis	April 11, 1961
—Quarter	10	Frank Ramsey vs. Minneapolis	April 4, 1959

MOST REBOUNDS
—Game	40	Bill Russell vs. Philadelphia	March 23, 1958
		Bill Russell vs. St. Louis	March 29, 1960
		Bill Russell vs. Los Angeles	April 18, 1962
—Half	25	Bill Russell vs. St. Louis	March 29, 1960
		Bill Russell vs. Los Angeles	April 18, 1962
—Quarter	19	Bill Russell vs. Los Angeles	April 18, 1962

MOST ASSISTS
—Game 19	19	Bob Cousy vs. St. Louis	April 9, 1957
		Bob Cousy at Minneapolis (St. Paul)	April 7, 1959
		Larry Bird vs New York	April 28, 1990
		Dennis Johnson vs. Los Angeles	June 7, 1985
		Bob Cousy vs. Cincinnati	April 10, 1963
		John Havlicek vs. Philadelphia	April 24, 1977
—Half	11		
—Quarter	8	Bob Cousy vs. St. Louis	April 9, 1957
		John Havlicek vs. Philadelphia	April 24, 1977

MOST PERSONAL FOULS
—Game	6	Many players	
—Half	6	Gene Conley vs. Syracuse	March 22, 1959
		Frank Ramsey vs. Syracuse	April 1, 1959
—Quarter	5	Greg Kite at Houston	June 1, 1986

MOST CONSECUTIVE FREE THROWS MADE
	56	Bill Sharman	March 18, 1959- April 9, 1959

THREE-POINT FIELD GOALS MADE
—Game	5	Danny Ainge vs. Los Angeles	June 11, 1987
	5	Larry Bird at Milwaukee	May 18, 1986
—Half	5	Danny Ainge vs. Los angeles	June 11, 1987
—Quarter	5	Danny Ainge vs. Los Angeles	June 11, 1987
—Game, no misses	4	Scott Wedman vs. Los Angeles	May 27, 1985

THREE-POINT FIELD GOALS ATTEMPTED
—Game	8	Danny Ainge at Detroit	May 28, 1988

MOST STEALS
—Game	7	Dennis Johnson vs. Atlanta	April 29, 1986

MOST BLOCKS
—Game	7	Robert Parish vs. Philadelphia	May 9, 1982

HIGHEST FIELD GOAL PERCENTAGE
—Game	1.000	Scott Wedman vs. Los Angeles (11-for-11)	May 27, 1985

Hall of Famer Tom Heinsohn.

TEAM PLAYOFF RECORDS

MOST POINTS
—Game	157	vs. New York	April 28, 1990
—Half	83	vs. New York	April 28, 1990
—Quarter	46	vs. St. Louis	March 27, 1960
	46	vs. Detroit	March 24, 1968

MOST FIELD GOALS MADE
—Game	63	vs. New York	April 28, 1990
—Half	34	vs. New York	April 28, 1990
—Quarter	21	vs. Los Angeles	April 18, 1965

MOST FIELD GOALS ATTEMPTED
—Game	140	vs. Syracuse	March 18, 1959
—Half	77	vs. Philadelphia	March 22, 1960
—Quarter	42	vs. Philadelphia	March 22, 1960

MOST FREE THROWS MADE
—Game	57	vs. Syracuse	March 21, 1953
—Half	21	vs. Cleveland	April 25, 1985
—Quarter	15	vs. Cleveland	April 25, 1985

MOST FREE THROWS ATTEMPTED
—Game	64	vs. Syracuse	March 21, 1953
—Half	30	vs. St. Louis	April 9, 1958
—Quarter	18	vs. Los Angeles	April 18, 1962

MOST REBOUNDS
—Game	107	vs. Philadelphia	March 19, 1960
—Half	60	vs. Philadelphia	March 19, 1960
—Quarter	31	vs. Philadelphia	March 19, 1960
		vs. Syracuse	March 23, 1961

MOST ASSISTS
—Game	46	vs. New York	April 28, 1990
—Half	28	vs. New York	April 28, 1990
—Quarter	15	vs. New York	April 28, 1990

MOST PERSONAL FOULS
—Game	52	vs. Syracuse	March 21, 1953
—Half	21	vs. Cincinnati	March 28, 1963
—Quarter	11	vs. Los Angeles	April 17, 1966

MOST DISQUALIFICATIONS
—Game	5	vs. Syracuse	March 21, 1953

MOST CONSECUTIVE WINS
	7	vs. three teams	May 6, 1986- May 29, 1986

MOST CONSECUTIVE LOSSES
	5	vs. Detroit	June 1, 1988- May 2, 1989

THREE-POINT FIELD GOALS MADE
—Game	8	at Milwaukee	May 18, 1986

THREE-POINT FIELD GOALS ATTEMPTED
—Game	12	at Detroit	May 28, 1988
	12	Milwaukee	May 18, 1986

MOST STEALS
—Game	15	vs. Houston	May 26, 1986
	15	Atlanta	April 29, 1986
	15	vs. New York	May 9, 1984
	15	at LA Lakers	June 6, 1984

MOST BLOCKS
—Game	15	at Washington	May 1, 1982

FEWEST TURNOVERS
—Game	5	vs. Chicago	April 26, 1987

Russell and Red.

CELTICS CAREER PLAYOFFS LEADERS

POINTS
1. John Havlicek — 3776
2. Larry Bird — 3559
3. Sam Jones — 2909
4. Bill Russell — 2673
5. Kevin McHale — 2603
6. Robert Parish — 2337
7. Tom Heinsohn — 2058
8. Bob Cousy — 2018
9. Dennis Johnson — 1733
10. Jo Jo White — 1720

AVERAGE POINTS (25 Game Min.)
1. Larry Bird — 24.5
2. John Havlicek — 22.0
3. Jo Jo White — 21.5
4. Tom Heinsohn — 19.8
5. Dave Cowens — 18.9
6. Sam Jones — 18.9
7. Kevin McHale — 18.7
8. Bill Sharman — 18.5
9. Bob Cousy — 18.5
10. Dennis Johnson — 16.7

GAMES PLAYED
1. John Havlicek — 172
2. Bill Russell — 165
3. Sam Jones — 154
4. Larry Bird — 145
5. Kevin McHale — 139
5. Robert Parish — 139
7. Don Nelson — 134
8. Tom Sanders — 130
9. Danny Ainge — 112
10. Bob Cousy — 109
10. K.C. Jones — 105

MINUTES PLAYED
1. Bill Russell — 7497
2. John Havlicek — 6860
3. Larry Bird — 6176
4. Robert Parish — 4902
5. Kevin McHale — 4729
6. Sam Jones — 4654
7. Bob Cousy — 4140
8. Dennis Johnson — 4096
9. Dave Cowens — 3768
10. Jo Jo White — 3428

FREE THROWS ATTEMPTED
1. Bill Russell — 1106
2. John Havlicek — 1046
3. Larry Bird — 925
4. Kevin McHale — 805
5. Bob Cousy — 799
6. Sam Jones — 753
7. Robert Parish — 625
8. Tom Heinsohn — 568
9. Dennis Johnson — 513
10. Frank Ramsey — 476

FREE THROWS MADE
1. John Havlicek — 874
2. Larry Bird — 825
3. Bill Russell — 667
4. Bob Cousy — 640
5. Kevin McHale — 628
6. Sam Jones — 611
7. Robert Parish — 469
8. Dennis Johnson — 429
9. Tom Heinsohn — 422
10. Frank Ramsey — 393

FREE THROW PERCENTAGE
(200 FTM Minimum)
1. Bill Sharman — .911 (370-406)
2. Larry Bird — .892 (825-925)
3. Dennis Johnson — .836 (429-513)
4. John Havlicek — .836 (874-1046)
5. Larry Siegfried — .834 (256-307)
6. Jo Jo White — .828 (256-309)
7. Frank Ramsey — .826 (393-476)
8. Don Nelson — .819 (385-470)
9. Sam Jones — .811 (611-753)
10. Bob Cousy — .801 (640-799)

ASSISTS
1. Bob Cousy — 937
2. Larry Bird — 932
3. John Havlicek — 825
4. Bill Russell — 770
5. Dennis Johnson — 711
6. Danny Ainge — 489
7. Jo Jo White — 452
8. K.C. Jones — 396
9. Sam Jones — 358
10. Dave Cowens — 333

FIELD GOALS ATTEMPTED
1. John Havlicek — 3329
2. Larry Bird — 2797
3. Sam Jones — 2571
4. Bill Russell — 2335
5. Tom Heinsohn — 2035
6. Bob Cousy — 2016
7. Robert Parish — 1804
8. Kevin McHale — 1747
9. Jo Jo White — 1629
10. Dave Cowens — 1627

FIELD GOALS MADE
1. John Havlicek — 1451
2. Larry Bird — 1331
3. Sam Jones — 1149
4. Bill Russell — 1003
5. Kevin McHale — 987
6. Robert Parish — 903
7. Tom Heinsohn — 818
8. Dave Cowens — 733
9. Jo Jo White — 732
10. Bob Cousy — 689

FIELD GOAL PERCENTAGE
(200 FGM Minimum)
1. Kevin McHale — .565 (987-1706)
2. Cedric Maxwell — .546 (356-652)
3. Robert Parish — .503 (934-1858)
4. Don Nelson — .500 (554-1109)
5. Bailey Howell — .498 (306-615)
6. Larry Bird — .476 (1331-2797)
7. Danny Ainge — .465 (479-1030)
8. Gerald Henderson — .454 (244-538)
9. Dave Cowens — .451 (733-1627)
10. Jo Jo White — .449 (732-1629)

REBOUNDS
1. Bill Russell — 4104
2. Larry Bird — 1379
3. Robert Parish — 1372
4. Dave Cowens — 1285
5. John Havlicek — 1186
6. Kevin McHale — 1046
7. Tom Heinsohn — 954
8. Tom Sanders — 763
9. Paul Silas — 763
10. Dennis Johnson — 739

PERSONAL FOULS
1. Bill Russell — 546
2. John Havlicek — 517
3. Tom Sanders — 508
4. Robert Parish — 480
5. Kevin McHale — 459
6. Larry Bird — 421
7. Tom Heinsohn — 417
8. Dave Cowens — 398
9. Sam Jones — 395
10. Frank Ramsey — 362

DISQUALIFICATIONS
1. Tom Sanders — 26
2. Dave Cowens — 15
3. Charlie Scott — 14
4. Tom Heinsohn — 14
5. Robert Parish — 14
6. Frank Ramsey — 13
7. Bailey Howell — 11
8. John Havlicek — 9
9. Bob Donham — 9
10. Bill Russell — 8
11. Jim Loscutoff — 8
12. Bob Brannum — 8
13. Kevin McHale — 8

INDIVIDUAL PLAYOFF PERFORMANCES

Scoring

54	John Havlicek, at Atlanta	April 1, 1973
51	Sam Jones, at New York	March 30, 1967
50	Bob Cousy, vs. Syracuse (4 OT)	March 21, 1953
47	Sam Jones, vs. Cincinnati	April 10, 1963

Field Goals Made

24	John Havlicek, at Atlanta	April 1, 1973
19	Sam Jones, at New York	March 30, 1967

Free Throws Made

30	Bob Cousy, vs. Syracuse (4 OT)	March 21, 1953
20	Bob Cousy, vs. Syracuse	March 17, 1954

Assists

19	Bob Cousy, vs. St. Louis	April 9, 1957
19	Bob Cousy, at Minneapolis	April 7, 1959
18	Bob Cousy, vs. Syracuse	March 18, 1959

Rebounds

40	Bill Russell, vs. Philadelphia	March 23, 1958
40	Bill Russell, vs. St. Louis	March 29, 1960
40	Bill Russell, vs. Los Angeles	April 18, 1962

OPPONENTS GREATEST INDIVIDUAL PLAYOFF PERFORMANCES

Scoring

63	Michael Jordan, Chicago at Boston (2OT)	April 20, 1986
61	Elgin Baylor, Los Angeles at Boston	April 14, 1962
53	Jerry West, at Los Angeles	April 23, 1969
50	Bob Pettit, at St. Louis	April 12, 1958
50	Wilt Chamberlain, Philadelphia at Boston	March 22, 1960
49	Michael Jordan, Chicago at Boston	April 17, 1986

Field Goals Made

22	Wilt Chamberlain, Philadelphia at Boston	March 22, 1960
22	Elgin Baylor, Los Angeles at Boston	April 14, 1962
22	Michael Jordan, Chicago at Boston	April 20, 1986

Free Throws Made

21	Oscar Robertson, Cincinnati at Boston	April 10, 1963
19	Bob Pettit, St. Louis at Boston	April 9, 1958

Assists

22	Glenn Rivers, at Atlanta	May 16, 1988
21	Earvin Johnson, at Los Angeles	June 3, 1984
20	Earvin Johnson, at Los Angeles	June 4, 1987
19	Earvin Johnson, at Los Angeles	June 14, 1987

Rebounds

41	Wilt Chamberlain, at Philadelphia	April 5, 1967
39	Wilt Chamberlain, at Philadelphia	April 6, 1965
38	Wilt Chamberlain, at San Francisco	April 24, 1964

Larry and Kevin anchored three championship teams in the 1980s.

CELTICS WORLD CHAMPIONSHIP TEAMS

1956-57
(44-28* regular season, 7-3 playoffs)
Coach: Red Auerbach
Bob Cousy (64 games), Tom Heinsohn (72), Dick Hemric (67), Jim Loscutoff (70), Jack Nichols (61), Togo Palazzi (20), Andy Phillip (67), Frank Ramsey (35), Arnie Risen (43), Bill Russell (48), Bill Sharman (67) and Lou Tsioropoulos (52). Trainer: Harvey Cohn.

1958-59
(52-20* regular season, 8-3 playoffs)
Coach: Red Auerbach
Gene Conley (50 games), Bob Cousy (65), Tom Heinsohn (66), K.C. Jones (49), Sam Jones (71), Jim Loscutoff (66), Frank Ramsey (72), Bill Russell (70), Bill Sharman (72), Ben Swain (58) and Lou Tsioropoulos (35). Trainer: Buddy LeRoux.

1959-60
(59-16* regular season, 8-5 playoffs)
Coach: Red Auerbach
Gene Conley (71 games), Bob Cousy (75), Gene Guarilia (48), Tom Heinsohn (75), K.C. Jones (74), Sam Jones (74), Maurice King (1), Jim Loscutoff (28), Frank Ramsey (73), John Richter (66), Bill Russell (74) and Bill Sharman (71). Trainer: Buddy LeRoux.

1960-61
(57-22* regular season, 8-5 playoffs)
Coach: Red Auerbach
Gene Conley (75 games), Bob Cousy (76), Gene Guarilia (25), Tom Heinsohn (74), K.C. Jones (78), Sam Jones (78), Jim Loscutoff (76), Frank Ramsey (79), Bill Russell (78), Tom Sanders (68) and Bill Sharman (61). Trainer: Buddy LeRoux.

1961-62
(62-20* regular season, 8-6 playoffs)
Coach: Red Auerbach
Carl Braun (48 games), Bob Cousy (75), Gene Guarilia (45), Tom Heinsohn (79), K.C. Jones (80), Sam Jones (78), Jim Loscutoff (76), Gary Phillips (67), Frank Ramsey (79), Bill Russell (76) and Tom Sanders (80). Trainer: Buddy LeRoux.

1962-63
(58-22* regular season, 8-5 playoffs)
Coach: Red Auerbach
Bob Cousy (76 games), Gene Guarilia (11), John Havlicek (80), Tom Heinsohn (76), K.C. Jones (79), Sam Jones (76), Jim Loscutoff (63), Clyde Lovellette (61), Frank Ramsey (77), Bill Russell (78), Tom Sanders (80) and Dan Swartz (39). Trainer: Buddy LeRoux.

1963-64
(59-21* regular season, 8-2 playoffs)
Coach: Red Auerbach
John Havlicek (80 games), Tom Heinsohn (76), K.C. Jones (80), Sam Jones (76), Jim Loscutoff (53), Clyde Lovellette (45), Johnny McCarthy (28), Willie Naulls (78), Frank Ramsey (75), Bill Russell (78), Tom Sanders (80) and Larry Siegfried (31). Trainer: Buddy LeRoux.

1964-65
(62-18* regular season, 8-4 playoffs)
Coach: Red Auerbach
Ron Bonham (37 games), Mel Counts (54), John Havlicek (75), Tom Heinsohn (67), K.C. Jones (78), Sam Jones (80), Willie Naulls (71), Bob Nordmann (3), Bill Russell (78), Tom Sanders (80), Larry Siegfried (72), John Thompson (64) and Gerry Ward (3). Trainer: Buddy LeRoux.

1965-66
(54-26, 2nd in East one game behind Philadelphia in regular season, 11-6 playoffs) Coach: Red Auerbach
Ron Bonham (39 games), Mel Counts (67), Sihugo Green (10), John Havlicek (71), K.C. Jones (80), Sam Jones (67), Willie Naulls (71), Don Nelson (75), Bill Russell (78), Tom Sanders (72), Woody Sauldsberry (39), Larry Siegfried (71), John Thompson (10) and Ron Watts (1). Trainer: Buddy LeRoux.

1967-68
(54-28, 2nd in East eight games behind Philadephia regular season; 12-7 in playoffs) Player-Coach: Bill Russell
Wayne Embry (78 games), Mal Graham (78), John Havlicek (82), Bailey Howell (82), Johnny Jones (51), Sam Jones (73), Don Nelson (82), Bill Russell (78), Tom Sanders (78), Larry Siegfried (62), Tom Thacker (65) and Rick Weitzman (25). Trainer: Joe DeLauri.

1968-69
(48-34, 4th in East nine games behind first-place Baltimore regular season; 12-6 in playoffs) Player-Coach: Bill Russell
Jim Barnes (49 games), Emmette Bryant (80), Don Chaney (20), Mal Graham (22), John Havlicek (82), Bailey Howell (78), Rich Johnson (31), Sam Jones (70), Don Nelson (82), Bud Olsen (7), Bill Russell (77), Tom Sanders (82) and Larry Siegfried (79). Trainer: Joe DeLauri.

1973-74
(56-26 regular season, 12-6 playoffs)
Coach: Tom Heinsohn

Assistant Coach: John Killilea
Don Chaney (81 games), Dave Cowens (80), Steve Downing (24), Henry Finkel (60), Phil Hankinson (28), John Havlicek (76), Steve Kuberski (78), Don Nelson (82), Paul Silas (82), Paul Westphal (82), Jo Jo White (82) and Art Williams (67). Trainer: Frank Challant. Assistant Trainer: Mark Volk.

1975-76
(54-28 regular season, 12-6 playoffs)
Coach: Tom Heinsohn
Assistant Coach: John Killilea
Jerome Anderson (22 games), Jim Ard (81), Tom Boswell (35), Dave Cowens (78), John Havlicek (76), Steve Kuberski (60), Glenn McDonald (75), Don Nelson (75), Charlie Scott (82), Ed Searcy (4), Paul Silas (81), Kevin Stacom (77) and Jo Jo White (82). Trainer: Frank Challant. Assistant Trainer: Mark Volk.

1980-81
(62-20** regular season, 12-5 playoffs)
Coach: Bill Fitch
Assistant Coaches: K.C. Jones and Jim Rodgers
Nate Archibald (80 games), Larry Bird (82), M.L. Carr (41), Terry Duerod (32), Eric Fernsten (45), Chris Ford (82), Gerald Henderson (82), Wayne Kreklow (25), Cedric Maxwell (81), Kevin McHale (82), Robert Parish (82) and Rick Robey (82). Trainer: Ray Melchiorre.

1983-84
(62-20* regular season, 15-8 playoffs)
Coach: K.C. Jones
Assistant Coaches: Jim Rodgers and Chris Ford
Danny Ainge (71 games), Larry Bird (79), Quinn Buckner (79), M.L. Carr (60), Carlos Clark (31), Gerald Henderson (78), Dennis Johnson (80), Greg Kite (35), Cedric Maxwell (80), Kevin McHale (82), Robert Parish (80) and Scott Wedman (68). Trainer: Ray Melchiorre.

1985-86
(67-15* regular season, 15-3 playoffs)
Coach: K.C. Jones
Assistant Coaches: Jim Rodgers and Chris Ford
Danny Ainge (80 games), Larry Bird (82), Rick Carlisle (77), Dennis Johnson (78), Greg Kite (64), Kevin McHale (68), Robert Parish (81), Jerry Sichting (82), David Thirdkill (49), Sam Vincent (57), Bill Walton (80), Scott Wedman (79) and Sly Williams (6), Trainer Ray Melchiorre.
*Best record in the NBA
**tied for best record in NBA

KC Jones and Scott Wedman celebrate the 1984 title.

1990-91 BOSTON CELTICS SCHEDULE

TELEVISION OUTLET

NOVEMBER - 1990

				Time	SpCh	WFXT	NBC	TNT
Fri	2	H	CLEVELAND	7:30	x			
Sat	3	A	NEW YORK	7:30		x		
Tue	6	A	CHICAGO	7:00		x		x
Fri.	9	H	CHICAGO	7:30	x			
Sat	10	A	NEW JERSEY	7:30		x		
Tue	13	A	MILWAUKEE	7:30		x		
Wed	14	H	CHARLOTTE	7:30	x			
Fri	16	H	UTAH	7:30	x			
Sat	17	A	WASHINGTON	7:30		x		
Wed	21	H	HOUSTON	7:30	x			
Fri	23	H	SACRAMENTO	7:30	x			
Sat	24	A	CLEVELAND	7:30		x		
Mon	26	*	MIAMI	7:30	x			
Wed	28	H	ATLANTA	7:30	x			
Fri	30	H	WASHINGTON	7:30	x			

DECEMBER - 1990

				Time	SpCh	WFXT	NBC	TNT
Sat	1	A	PHILADELPHIA	7:30	x			
Mon	3	H	SEATTLE	7:30	x			
Wed	5	H	DENVER	7:30	x			
Fri	7	A	DALLAS	7:00		x		x
Sat	8	A	SAN ANTONIO	7:30		x		
Mon	10	A	HOUSTON	7:30		x		
Wed	12	H	MILWAUKEE	7:30	x			
Fri	14	H	DETROIT	8:00	x			x
Sat	15	A	MIAMI	7:30		x		
Wed	19	H	PHILADELPHIA	7:30	x			
Thu	20	A	CHARLOTTE	7:30		x		
Wed	26	H	INDIANA	7:30	x			
Fri	28	A	ATLANTA	8:00		x		

JANUARY - 1991

				Time	SpCh	WFXT	NBC	TNT
Wed	2	H	NEW YORK	8:00	x			x
Fri	4	H	PHOENIX	7:30	x			
Sun	6	H	DALLAS	7:30	x			
Tue	8	A	NEW YORK	7:30		x		
Wed	9	H	MILWAUKEE	7:30	x			
Fri	11	H	LA CLIPPERS	7:30	x			
Sat	12	A	WASHINGTON	7:30		x		
Wed	16	H	GOLDEN STATE	7:30	x			
Fri	18	H	NEW JERSEY	7:30	x			
Mon	21	A	DETROIT	7:30		x		
Wed	23	H	DETROIT	8:00	x			x
Fri	25	A	PHILADELPHIA	7:30	x			
Sun	27	H	LA LAKERS	12:30			x	
Mon	28	A	MINNESOTA	7:00		x		
Wed	30	H	ORLANDO	7:30	x			

FEBRUARY - 1991

				Time	SpCh	WFXT	NBC	TNT
Fri	1	A	CHARLOTTE	7:30		x		
Sun	3	H	WASHINGTON	1:00	x			
Wed	6	H	CHARLOTTE	7:30	x			
Thu	7	A	NEW YORK	7:30		x		
Tue	12	A	SEATTLE	7:00		x		
Thu	14	A	GOLDEN STATE	7:30		x		
Fri	15	A	LA LAKERS	7:30		x		x
Sun	17	A	DENVER	2:00		x		
Tue	19	A	PHOENIX	6:00		x		x
Fri	22	*	NEW JERSEY	7:30	x			
Sun	24	A	INDIANA	1:00			x	
Tue	26	A	CHICAGO	7:30		x		
Wed	27	H	MINNESOTA	7:30	x			

MARCH - 1991

				Time	SpCh	WFXT	NBC	TNT
Fri	1	H	SAN ANTONIO	8:00	x			x
Sun	3	H	PORTLAND**	TBA	x		x	
Mon	4	*	INDIANA	7:30	x			
Wed	6	H	MIAMI	7:30	x			
Fri	8	A	LA CLIPPERS	7:30		x		
Sun	10	A	PORTLAND	7:00		x		
Tue	12	A	SACRAMENTO	7:30		x		
Wed	13	A	UTAH	7:00		x		x
Fri	15	A	WASHINGTON	8:00		x		
Sun	17	H	PHILADELPHIA	12:00			x	
Tue	19	A	ATLANTA	8:00		x		
Wed	20	H	WASHINGTON	7:30	x			
Fri	22	A	INDIANA	7:30		x		
Thu	28	A	MIAMI	7:30		x		
Fri	29	H	CLEVELAND	8:00	x			x
Sun	31	H	CHICAGO	12:30			x	

APRIL - 1991

				Time	SpCh	WFXT	NBC	TNT
Tue	2	A	NEW JERSEY	7:30		x		
Thu	4	H	NEW JERSEY	7:30	x			
Sat	6	A	ORLANDO	7:30		x		
Thu	11	A	MILWAUKEE	7:30		x		
Fri	12	H	MIAMI	7:30	x			
Sun	14	H	NEW YORK	1:00			x	
Tue	16	A	DETROIT	7:30		x		
Thu	18	A	PHILADELPHIA	7:30	x			
Fri	19	A	CLEVELAND	8:00		x		
Sun	21	H	ATLANTA	1:00	x			

* An asterisk denotes a home game in Hartford, CT.

** - Possible change to exclusive broadcast on NBC-TV.

All games on WEEI (590 AM) radio.

All times are local times, and are all "PM".